Bulw
Occult Personality

A Graphic Introduction
by
John S Moore

Design and formatting by Alistair Moore

MANDRAKE

First Edition

Published by Mandrake

Acknowledgements

My mother, in whose book of ghost stories I was early fascinated by *The Haunted and Haunters*.

Michael Neve who first suggested I should write about Bulwer.

Henry Cobbold of Knebworth EBL's great, great, great grandson and

Jill Campbell his archivist who provided images and information.

Alistair Moore my son who did the formatting.

John Higgins who let me reuse his illustrations, (marked with JH).

Paul Campbell who produced new ones of his own, (marked with PC).

Charles Tattersall & Oliver Ball who did proof reading.

Mogg Morgan (my publisher) who designed the cover.

Other Books by John Moore
Aleister Crowley: A Modern Master
Crowley: A Beginners Guide

Contents

Introduction

Edward Bulwer, Lord Lytton, once the most successful novelist in the English speaking world, now unfairly neglected and even derided, was also the central figure in the underground culture of magic and the occult. With his esoteric studies he built a reputation for deep learning in the history and philosophy of this alternative tradition, as well as passing for an adept in his own right. His creative influence, especially through his occult fiction, was surprisingly far reaching.

The book sets the achievement of this nineteenth century magus into a large historical context, exploring the intellectual and other influences on him as well as movements he inspired. Some chapters discuss aspects of Bulwer's life, while some explore people and ideas that influenced him and others those he influenced. His seminal role in a several cultural movements has been largely forgotten, not least in his home country. This book offers an often unfamiliar perspective on the Victorian era and hopefully succeeds in provoking some questions about our own times.

Knebworth

Visitors to Knebworth House in Hertfordshire can expect to be impressed by such noteworthy features as the banqueting hall with its Jacobean oak screen and the high Victorian gothic seating in the state drawing room.

The powerful presence of Edward Bulwer-Lytton pervades the whole. In his study we see a portrait of him with his long pipe.

His comes across as an enviable way of life. We see his tarot pack and display of old occult books. I like to think of the magical influence on the house. He is said to have been a pupil of Eliphas Lévi, who first gave the occult interpretation of these traditional French playing cards. Bulwer's occult interests add something vital to this building, so largely his creation. It gives an esoteric significance which raises the Victorian gothic above what it so often is: a pious romantic Pre-Raphaelite Christian fantasy. The element of the occult put seriously into romanticism changes and elevates it. No longer is it fiction, no longer escapism. It sits well with the sense of a great house and an old family.

The way he influenced the course of the culture is itself like that of a magus. And the dismissal of his ideas is more confirmation of their esoteric status. Yet it should be remembered that his occult personality may not entirely coincide with his real one.

His life

Born in 1803, well enough educated without passing through the ordeal of English public school, he went up to Trinity College Cambridge there to begin his career as man of fashion.

Though strictly speaking the Regency ended with the death of George III and the accession of George IV, what is popularly called the Regency era lasted for some years after that, and young Bulwer qualifies as a Regency dandy.

Disapproving of his marriage, his mother cut off his allowance, so he began writing to finance his fashionable lifestyle.

After Dickens he was the most famous novelist of his day. At forty years old, with the death of his mother, he inherited Knebworth House and rebuilt it in an extravagant gothic style. His political career culminated in his appointment as Secretary of State for the Colonies in 1858. He was offered the throne of Greece but declined.

For his literary and political achievements, he was ennobled in 1866.

His life

For forty years he was known as Bulwer, for twenty-two, having added his mother's surname, Bulwer-Lytton, and the last seven as Lord Lytton.

He had one disastrous marriage, to Rosina née Wheeler, a strong willed Irish woman, and two legitimate children, Emily who died somewhat mysteriously aged nineteen, and Robert, who wrote poems under the name of Owen Meredith, and was to become Viceroy of India.

He died in 1873 and is buried in St Edmund's chapel in Westminster Abbey.

LORD LYTTON

Byron
1788-1824

LORD BYRON

The young Bulwer had a personal link with Lord Byron (1788 –1824), through his warm relationship with the scandalous Lady Caroline Lamb, who lived at Brockett Hall, not far from Knebworth. Married to prime minister Lord Melbourne, she was famous for her very public affair with the poet, and for a dinner party at the Hall when she served herself up naked in a soup tureen as a birthday present for her husband.

His *Pelham* is said to have ended the fashion for Byronism. Still, Byron was his hero, and the prototype for his earliest fiction is said to have been the last books of Byron's epic *Don Juan*. He pioneered the novel of fashion, a style christened by Hazlitt "silver fork". The eventual masterpiece of the genre was Thackeray's *Vanity Fair*.

The silver fork novel metamorphosed into the Newgate novel, all about crime and villainy. The masterpiece of this genre was to be Dickens' *Oliver Twist*. Bulwer believed that crime can reveal deep truths about human nature. Mario Praz says that Bulwer tamed and diluted the Byronic villain for the bourgeois age. His *Ernest Maltravers* is a Byronic figure though not a villain.

In its egoism and aristocratic radicalism the Byronism of the 1820s prefigured the Nietzscheanism of the 1890s. In *England and the English* 1831, Bulwer looks

4

Byron
1788-1824

for the causes of the cult of Byronic melancholy. With the increase of commerce and prosperity aristocratic influence, with "*constant vying*" and "*consequent mortification*" had been steadily increasing throughout society. Hence English reserve and discontent.

The effect of peace after the recent war led the public to reflect on these features of national character. Another factor was that the 1820s were still impressed by the meteoric career of Napoleon, "*the modern Alexander*" which brought a taste for adventure. Byron's writing and character, even his appearance, perfectly expressed the national mood.

By 1830 the public had had its fill of this mood. Politically the early 1830s was the era of reform. However, Byronic and aristocratic attitudes still persisted in some quarters.

Bulwer concludes that Byron's genius had been overrated. Disowning his early admiration, he followed and partly led the times in finding a new hero in Jeremy Bentham. When he first entered parliament he was an enthusiastic reformer.

Later in his career he seems to have modified his views, and parts of *King Arthur*, his epic poem of 1851, are unmistakably Byronic.

Reform

Bulwer was very much an Englishman of his time. In his writing we have a window into an earlier form of radicalism than that which is generally familiar. Sometimes freedom goes out of vogue for a season. In his *England and the English*, published on the eve of the Victorian age, he writes of certain old fashioned people who still bang on about liberty and America. By 1830 liberty was a passion of the past, an old cause. The new cause was philosophical radicalism.

Though less well known than 1848, let alone 1789, 1830 was also a revolutionary year. In France the recently restored Bourbons were overthrown and the citizen king Louis Philippe came to power. Belgium achieved independence from the Netherlands. There was a Polish revolt against Russian rule. In England, following Catholic emancipation, there was vigorous agitation for electoral reform.

We can read the eighteenth century novelists to see what Bulwer meant when he criticised the influence of aristocracy on English society. Now that is long faded we may consider what has replaced it. History can reveal features of our own society that may otherwise pass unnoticed. At this time Europe lived in the shadow of the French Revolution. For British reformers, utilitarianism and philosophical radicalism provided a self-assured body of doctrine.

The important cause for Bulwer at this time is political reform. From this point of view it was necessary to move away from Byronic and aristocratic attitudes.

As he saw it these involved a cynicism that would have sneered at the youthful enthusiasms of 1830. He attributes many English traits to the effects of aristocratic power, ascribing all distinctive national character to the constitution. Later developments would show whether he was right. Once aristocratic power had gone, English character should have changed radically. If it didn't less may depend so completely on the political constitution as he bluntly asserts at this time.

Surprisingly he was still hailing the recent end of an aristocratic literary patronage that Dr Johnson was welcoming some decades earlier.

Bentham
1748 –1832

THE GREATEST HAPPINESS OF THE GREATEST NUMBER.

JEREMY BENTHAM

Bentham's utilitarianism was a large part of British philosophical radicalism, a self assured body of political and economic doctrine whose heyday coincided with the middle class coming to power in France in the 1830 revolution. Like socialists of a later era, philosophical radicals held that their new order could resolve all discontents, and coercion would not be felt once change has been effected.

Bentham was the decisive influence on nineteenth century judicial reform. His target was the jurist **William Blackstone** (1723–1780), with his concern for traditional safeguards, and warnings about the dangers of government. Bentham was more concerned with getting rid of the **bloody code**, which prescribed hanging for a great number of relatively minor offences.

England and the English shows the Victorian project at its inception. Bulwer makes it sound reasonable; the flaws came out later. When we look back we may not see the rational project, tending to think of Victorian

Eccentric enlightener Jeremy Bentham's most important project was to reform the criminal code. He himself was grounded in eighteenth century prejudice about liberty, and would not have envisaged the full revolutionary use that would later be made of his ideas. For his purpose the greatest happiness principle was a useful rational formula, not a tool for transforming the whole culture. It was partly intended to supply a meaning to moral terms like "ought", "good", "evil", "right" and "wrong", which, he says, otherwise have none.

...HANGED BY THE NECK UNTIL YOU ARE DEAD!

Bentham

1748 –1832

values as something needful to escape. *England and the English* contains in a sense the programme for the era which was to come. Though generally favourable to Bentham, Bulwer puts the following objection:-

"In his list of motives, though he includes sympathy, he omits conscience, or the feeling of duty: one would never imagine from reading him that any human being ever did an act merely because it is right, or abstained from it merely because it is wrong".

Bentham did not overlook this, he was deliberate, for him the idea of the purely moral character required further analysis.

For Bentham there should be no punishment of an offence if it is not injurious, to someone.

> *Cases in which punishment is groundless.*
> *XIII.4*
> *These are,*
> *IV. I. Where there has never been any mischief: where no mischief has been produced to any body by the act in question.*

In his epic poem *King Arthur* Bulwer pokes fun at the greatest happiness principle by employing it as the Danish king's argument to justify cannibalism as he prepared to eat Gawain.

After his death, following his own request, Bentham was stuffed, and his body can still be seen on the staircase at University College London.

Victorianism

Some hearts may sink at the sight of a bookshelf with a complete set of Lord Lytton's books next, perhaps, to a shelf of Macaulay's histories. Take out a volume and you may find its pages are still uncut. They seem to represent a taste and a mentality that has gone, and that sums up the Victorians. They can find themselves among those books sold by the yard to decorate pubs.

As Bulwer articulates it the Victorian project was rational enough, but when we look back on it we may see instead irrational convention that was hard to escape, prudery, hypocrisy and limited idea of the feminine. It was Bulwer's grand-godson, cynical Bloomsburyite Lytton Strachey, who did most to ruin the reputation of the Victorians generally.

WITH NATIONS, AS WITH INDIVIDUALS, IT IS NECESSARY TO RETURN TO PAST EMOTIONS IN ORDER TO JUDGE OF THE MERITS OF PAST APPEALS TO THEM.

JH

Though in his proto-Victorian synthesis Bulwer does foresee the evils a later age would identify in Victorianism, they are outweighed by other factors. He sees good in religion and the established church.

Victorianism

The rejection of eighteenth century egoism marked the onset of a new era. It is conventional to associate this with the rise of the middle classes, but another factor was the influence of Prussia. Bulwer shows admiration for Prussia with its absolute state. Unlike most of his countrymen he did not object to conscription.

deep ideas he includes sops to the public, like *"purifying"* the love of King Harold and Edith Swan-Neck, which he insists was chaste and unconsummated.

Like his friend Dickens, Bulwer accepted he had to work with the sentimental prejudices of his public. Unlike Thackeray he did not chafe at this. Like Dickens he could mix in serious instruction. So among a few

The Occult

At its best the occult is less about performing miracles than unexpected sources of wisdom. To its devotees the tradition is a hidden creative power, defying and subverting the official doctrines of the age. Change does not always mean progress. As much deep learning has been forgotten, it is questionable that we moderns really have a wisdom that is so satisfying to all impulses as what has sometimes existed in the past.

At the turn of the seventeenth century, John Donne and John Dee expressed different types of religious consciousness. Donne, concerned about death, desired salvation. From sensuality to piety was a common enough transition. The accents of his religious poems are not so different from those of his sensual ones, given his premises:- *love death, fear, hope.*

There was a different kind of religion available, that of the occult philosopher. His object is to offer fulfilment for all kinds of hard to satisfy desires. The spiritual balance esteemed by the magus comes from a continuous awareness of possibilities and the need to keep them open.

He reminds himself that any condition of mind in which he may happen to find himself is at best a partial truth.

Many people are interested in the occult, what do they or could they get out of it?

The occultist's view of man is an ultra-romantic one, concerned with the most ambitious magical type of desires. These are not necessarily to be taken quite literally, but certainly not simply allegorically. For him life as a business of trying to satisfy these ambitions or what would happily be accepted as equivalent substitutes.

The desires set the pitch of the type of satisfaction aimed at. In reaching such satisfaction, in effecting the substitution, great variety of concepts and categories will come into play. From this point of view everything you encounter is symbolic, with at least a surface and a deeper meaning.

The Occult

All esoteric literature has to be read between the lines. You are introduced to a world of symbols from which to create a personal mythology, and expected to learn to read it in relation to your own objectives. There is ambiguity in all symbols; no clear instruction can be given as to how to achieve the desired object. Surrounded by conflicting interpretations you must cultivate the ability to read the world symbolically. Those who aspire to secret knowledge take nothing at face value.

Dee's creative synthesis blended astrology. English nationalism, Arthurian legend, the Astraea myth, Enochian magic and occult imperialism. He was an esoteric powerhouse of key importance to his times. Significantly he worked as a spy. The concern with secret power and influence extends to an interest in espionage, a common theme in the life of the occultist.

The economic theory that underlay philosophical radicalism was the kind of science to give **William Blake** the horrors, a materialistic and very exoteric teaching.

BACON'S PHILOSOPHY HAS RUINED ENGLAND.

It promotes human happiness in its own way, but on a general rather than an individual level. Its aims are quite different from occult science except insofar as happiness is the end. To acquire personal wealth, to enrich one's nation, to build factories, exploit labour and agriculture, certainly this brings happiness, though not for all. Power increasing is happiness. But happiness can take different, subtle contemplative forms, all quite relative to the individual, and these occult science taps.

The Occult

In the nature of things one would not expect much solid evidence that it was ever successful. In *The Last of the Barons*, Warner, the royal alchemist, has invented a prototype steam engine, which he calls his Eureka. It has the potential to change the world, but arouses only suspicion and gets destroyed and forgotten.

Many centuries earlier **Hero of Alexandria** (10 – 70 AD) had invented a steam engine. We conjecture that many highly original discoveries in natural science were made by the ancient Alexandrians, about which records have been lost.

How much more with the peculiarly internal nature of the aspirations to which occult science speaks? Occultism necessarily talks in riddles, it imposes barriers, limits, and threatens dire penalties which must not be taken at face value, though it may be dangerous to disregard them at face value too.

There are dangers and follies intrinsic to the occult. There is a close affinity between magic and psychedelic experience, even schizophrenia. The value of ritual magic must depend on there being real wisdom somewhere contained in its procedures. The history of most of the offshoots is of greed, power and spiritual arrogance of those with a little knowledge, who have developed some extraordinary but elementary ability like the capacity to have visions.

The best ideas get corrupted. There is no copyright on thought and anyone can construct his own religions and philosophies with whatever materials are to hand. Divested of their background, the ideas and images which promise enlightenment and liberation harden into superstitions, and turn into vehicles for crude personal ambition.

The danger of degrading the mystery is one of the best reasons for writing in a cryptic, esoteric style. In speaking of the philosophy, there is the almost insuperable difficulty of keeping it pure. Even in trying to explain these things I can hardly help profaning them. This is inevitable when attempting to write lucidly about matters that are normally and traditionally discussed obliquely.

Occult Reading

I KNOW BY EXPERIENCE THAT THOSE WIZARD OLD BOOKS ARE FULL OF HOLES AND PITFALLS. I MYSELF ONCE FELL INTO ONE AND REMAINED THERE 45 DAYS AND 3 HOURS WITHOUT FOOD, CRYING FOR HELP AS LOUD AS I COULD, BUT NOBODY CAME. YOU MAY BELIEVE THAT OR NOT JUST AS YOU PLEASE, BUT ITS TRUE.

JH

With his reading in this field Bulwer made himself into one of the most learned occult scholars in Europe. But he was much more than just a scholar. He learning was to inspire not just his fiction but aspects of his personality and ambition. Early on he stated his intention to study Albertus Magnus and Cornelius Agrippa, which he presumably proceeded to do. That would have been just a start. Here is a list of his books. We can't say how many of them he actually read, but the knowledge he acquired was impressively wide ranging.

Agrippa, Henry Cornelius.
Fourth Book of Occult Philosophy and Geomancy. Magical Elements of Peter de Abano. Astronomical Geomancy: The Nature of Spirits and Arbatel of Magic.

Anon.
A Glimpse of the Great Secret Society

Anon.
A Suggestive enquiry into the Hermetic Mystery
1872

Anon
The Athenian Oracle an entire collection of all the valuable questions and answers. (4 volumes all complete) 1703

Anon.
Lineis Mon Tibus Et Tuberculis Manus Constitutonem Hominium and Fortunae vires Oftendentes.
1663

Anon
Chymica Vannus.
1666

Anon.
Hermippus Redivivus. Or the Sage's Triumph Over Old Age and the Grave.
1771

Anon.
The Conjurors Magazine or Magical and Physiognomical Mirror.(3 volumes all complete)

Anon The Mysteries of Magic 1728

Anon Tabule Chiromanticae 1613

Aubrey, John.
Miscellanies upon Various Subjects. 1784

Bond, William
The Supernatural Philosopher, or The Mysteries of Magick, the Life and Surprising Adventures of Mr Duncan Campbell. 1728

Occult Reading

Brewster. Sir David.
Letters on Natural Magic addressed to Sir Walter Scott.
1838

Edited by T. Brown Familiar Letters, written by ... John
late Earl of Rochester, and several other persons of
honour and quality. 1697

John Bulwer Chirologia 1644
Bulweri, Johannes.
Man Transformed or the Artificial Changeling. 1650

Burthogge, Richard.
An Essay upon Reason and the Nature of Spirits. 1694

Capern, Thomas.
The Mighty Curative Powers of Mesmerism.

Case, John.
The Angelical Guide Shewing Men and Women their
Lott or Chance in this elementary Life.(1 volume of an
original set of 4, only 1 recorded in 1971) 1697

Cattan, Christopher.
The Geomancie of Master Christopher Cattan
Gentleman. 1591

Coley Henry Clavis Astrologiæ Elimata; or, a Key to the
whole Art of Astrologie, 1676

Davies, Sir John.
The Original Nature and Immortality of the Soul, A
Poem. 1697

Davis, Andrew Jackson.
The Principles of Nature Her Divine Revelations and A
Voice to Mankind (2 volumes all complete) 1847

Davis, Andrew, Jackson.
The Great Harmonia (3 volumes all complete) 1851

Dee Dr. John.

Occult Reading

A True and Faithful Relation of What Passed Between Dr. John Dee..... and Some Spirits. Preface by Meric Casuabon D.D. 1659

Digby's Of Bodies 1645

Ennemoser, Joseph.
The History of Magic. Translated from the German by William Howitt.(2 volumes all complete) 1865

J.S.F. Demonologia, or Natural Knowledge explained being an Expose of ancient and Modern Superstitions. 1827

Gaffarel, James. Translated by Edmund Chilmead. Unheard of Curiosities Concerning the Talismanical Sculpture of the Persians. The Horoscope of the Patriarkes and the Reading of the Stars. 1650

Glanvill on Witches 1531

Heydon John
Theomagia or the Temple of Wisdome. (only 1 volume, this volume listed as missing in the 71 survey) 1664

Iamblichus on The Mysteries of the Egyptians Chaldeans and Assyrians. 1821

Kerner, Justinus.
The Seeress of Prevorst, being Revelations Concerning the Inner life of Man. Translated from the German by Mrs Crowe. 1845

Lebrun, Pierre.
Histoire Critique Des Pratiques Superstitieuses (4 volumes all complete) 1642

L'Estrange. R.O.
Twenty Two select Colloquies out of Erasmus Roterodamus pleasantly Representing several Superstitious Lévities that were cresp into the Church of Rome in His Days. 1689

Lilly, William.
An Introduction to Astrology. 1835

Lilly, Will.
Supernatural Sights and Apparitions seen in London June 30 1644 interpreted with a mathematical Discourse of the now imminent conjunction of Jupiter and Mars 26th July 1644. The effects which either here or some neere counties from thence may be expected. 1644

Nostradamus, Michel De.
The Works of Nostradamus. 1656

Ouvaroff M.
Mysteries of the Eleusis. 1817

An Oxonian.
Thaumaturgia. Or Elucidations of the Marvellous. 1835

Peruchio.
La Chiromance, La Physionomie et La Geomance. (2 volumes all complete) 1656

Philalethes, Eugenius. F.R.S.
Long Livers A Curious History of Such Persons of Both Sexes who have Lived Several Ages and Grown Young Again with the Rare Secret of Rejuvenescency of

Occult Reading

Arnoldus de Villa Nova. 1722

Salomon. Rabbi.
Les Clavicutes de Rabbi Salomon.

Michael Sendivogius A New Light of Alchymy 1674

E. Sibley, MD
Claudius Ptolemy together with the Arabian Authors on
the Doctrine of the Nativities 1796

George Sinclair Natural Philosophy Improven by New
Experiments 1683

Smedley, Taylor, Thomson, Rich.
Encyclopaedia Metropolitana, or System of Universal
Knowledge. 1855

Jacobus de STRADA Epitome Thesauri Antiquitatum
1553
Swedenborg, Emanuel.
A Treatise Concerning Heaven and Hell and the

Wonderful Things Therein as Heard and Seen by the
Honorable and Learned Emanuel Swedenborg.

Todd, Thompson. Anthony.(editor)
The Occult Sciences the Philosophy of Magic Prodigies
and Apparent Miracles.(2 volumes all complete)

Townshend Rev. Chauncey Hare.
Facts in Mesmerism. 1848

Wilkins, John.
Mathematical Magick or the Wonders that may be
preformed by Mechanical Geometry. 1691

Wilson, James. Translated from the copy of Leo
Allatius, The Tetrabiblos or the Quadripartite of
Ptolemy.

Scholarship

> **He was said to have studied deeply that knowledge which the philosophers of old called 'occult'.**

Bulwer's reading was wide and deep. While his knowledge offered a window into obscure corners of history, he would do more than regale ancient tradition. He applied his learning, and the impulse he received from it was creative and in its own way progressive.

He had become one of the most well read men in Europe in the traditions of the occult. Hints from his novels formed the basis for a serious magical revival, which was to feed into the symbolist movement in European art and literature.

Bulwer had a good grounding in the classics, and was also conversant with other mythologies, like the Norse and the Celtic. He inspired a quest for religious wisdom that would not stick with familiar frameworks, but eagerly absorbed the discoveries of archaeologists and historians.

In the years that followed, much more was to be learned about Egyptians and Chaldeans, as well as the Mahayana Buddhists whose bodhisattva ideals fitted so well into Rosicrucian teaching about the Great White Brotherhood. With everything that was discovered about alien civilisations there was so much more material for theosophising.

Following his example there were not a few Victorian men and women happy to spend their time pondering over *many a quaint and curious volume of forgotten lore*, often achieving a solid depth of learning.

Frequently, too, they were not content to remain mere scholars, they wanted to apply their knowledge; they would create, found movements, write rituals, develop their personalities.

Bulwer with his pipe, sketched by Daniel Maclise in the early 1830s.

> *"We have long learned to reverence the fine intellect of Bulwer. We take up any production of his pen with a positive certainty that, in reading it, the wildest passions of our nature, the most profound of our thoughts, the brightest visions of our fancy, and the most ennobling and lofty of our aspirations will, in due turn, be enkindled within us. We feel sure of rising from the perusal a wiser if not a better man. In no instance are we deceived"* (Poe).

> *We have heard it alleged with some evidence that the prominence given to intellectual power in Bulwer's romances has proved a main stimulus to mental culture in thousands of young men in England and America.* (Emerson).

The Tradition

Academic philosophy does not typically give access to what the mystics call higher metaphysics, but it need not contradict it. In Wittgenstein's terminology they are different language games. Those who think mystic enlightenment is the real task of philosophy might be tempted to rank Iamblichus and Hermes Trismegistus as the greatest philosophers of antiquity. Bulwer did not take this path. He did not denigrate mainstream philosophy. In one place or another he cited most of the major philosophers and many lesser known ones. His study of the occult masters involved no conflict with this.

Iamblichus
245 – c. 325

Iamblichus on The Mysteries of the Egyptians Chaldeans and Assyrians, 1821.

It was Iamblichus the neoplatonist, one of the founding fathers of esotericism in the west who connected up the religious wisdom of the east with Greek philosophy. In the imaginative atmosphere of the early centuries of the Roman Empire Iamblichus brought in theosophical traditions from the orient. A lot of these involved cosmologies, bizarre descriptions of the universe.

The last great pagan philosopher of the ancient world was **Proclus**, who devised an elaborate mystical metaphysics. This was Christianised by **Pseudo-Dionysius** from where it passed into the highly original system of the Irish **John Scotus Eriugena** to inspire a long tradition of western occultism.

Psellus
1017-1078

In Constantinople a continuous Christian neoplatonic tradition flourished for some centuries. Distinguished philosopher and historian Michael Psellus led an eleventh century classical revival which influenced the arts. He sought to reconcile paganism and Christianity, and for the first time for centuries some people began to take the pagan gods seriously again. He commented on the *Chaldean Oracles*, as did his fifteenth century successor Plethon, who attributed them to Zoroaster.

The Tradition

Albertus Magnus
1200-1280

"You will remember that Albertus Magnus, after describing minutely the process by which spirits may be invoked and commanded, adds emphatically that the process will instruct and avail only to the few - that a man must be born a magician! - that is, born with a peculiar physical temperament, as a man is born a poet. Rarely are men in whose constitution lurks this occult power of the highest order of intellect - usually in the intellect there is some twist, perversity, or disease." (The Haunted and the Haunters)

Some historians view the scholastic philosopher Albertus as greater and more original than his pupil **Aquinas**.

There was a legend that the Virgin Mary promised Albertus Magnus supremacy in philosophy, but punished his arrogance with the oblivion of Alzheimer's three years before his death.

Bulwer would have read about Albertus in Isaac Disraeli's Curiosities of Literature:-

Albertus Magnus entertained the Earl of Holland, as that Earl passed through Cologne, in a severe winter, with a warm summer scene, luxuriant in fruits and flowers The fact is related by Trithemius — and this magical scene connected with his vocal head, and his books De Secretis Mulierum, and De Mirabilus, confirmed the accusations they raised against the great Albert for being a magician. His apologist, Theophilns Raynaud, is driven so hard to defend Albertus, that he at once asserts the winter changed to summer and the speaking head to he two infamous flams! He will not believe these authenticated facts, although he credits a miracle which proves the sanctity of Albertus, — after three centuries, the body of Albert the Great remained as sweet as ever !

Plethon
1360-1454

Born George Gemistos, this neoplatonist adopted the name of Plethon, because it sounded like Plato. Based at Mystra near the site of ancient Sparta, he lived in the last days before the fall of Constantinople to the Turks.

The Tradition

Ruins of Mystra

He came to Florence in 1439 in an unsuccessful attempt to heal the schism between the eastern and western churches. There he met Marsilio Ficino, and brought Greek learning to the west. If there was one person who consciously willed to produce the Italian renaissance, it was he.

Plethon himself was uninterested in art. Yet art is one of the forms in which philosophy may survive, as

renaissance platonism could and did. Platonism in the west had a vitalising creative effect, recapturing something of the life affirming spirit of the ancients. Even Proclus is genuine Greek tradition. The Greeks back to Homer and beyond are the root of western civilisation. Neoplatonism helped to clarify a somewhat anti-Christian tendency.

We may see Plethon as a religious thinker. He wrote pagan hymns which are however said to show no religious feeling. He is recorded as saying that in a few years Christianity would be replaced by a new religion, which would be the neopagan one that he had just invented. This involved a trinity of Zeus, Poseidon and Hera. All the gods lived in harmony and filial obedience to their father Zeus. They were thus very different from the lustful and amoral gods of Homer. In his new religion he taught polygamy, the temporal infinity of the universe and that human souls would be reincarnated an infinite number of times.

According to Plethon's orthodox opponent, **Scholarios** (1400 -1473) who was to become Patriarch of Constantinople under the Turks, Plethon's teacher was one **Elissaeus**, a Jew who had become a pagan and was burnt at the stake. He in turn is said to have been influenced by the Iranian mystic **Suhrawardi**, who drew Platonic and Zoroastrian themes into his Sufistic theosophy.

The Tradition

Ficino
1433- 1499

Plethon brought with him to Florence some works of Plato previously unknown to the west. Before tackling these, Ficino was asked by **Cosimo de Medici** to translate some writings attributed to Hermes Trismegistus, which he had also received. Under such influences Ficino developed a neoplatonic philosophy of his own and became one of the most influential philosophers of the Italian renaissance.

Ficino saw himself as a link in the great chain of Platonists, which included **Hermes**, **Zoroaster**, **Plato**, **Plotinus**, **Iamblichus** and more lately **Nicholas Cusanus** (1401 –1464). The philosophy lent itself to visualisation in the form of diagrams, simplifications for practical use. The neoplatonic mystic aspired towards the most desirable state, in the context of various imaginary cosmologies and pedigrees of wisdom, re-echoing the atmosphere in which the ancient world had moved to Christianity.

Ficino's interest was strongly aroused by some of the magical practices described in the hermetic corpus, invoking the help of what the ancients called demons. With questionable orthodoxy he linked the astrological intelligences called on by the pagans to the angelology of Christian fathers.

For Ficino there is no sudden elevation to a transcendental insight, but it can be approached by small steps. The soul was the mid point of reality, the intermediary of all things.

Ficino's optimism marks a difference from the pessimism of ancient neoplatonists. He upheld the idea of the perfection of nature, rather than the need for its salvation, and had much to say of the bond of love. He said the trouble with the pleasures of the senses is not that they are pleasures, but that they do not last. His pupil **Pico de Mirandola** (1463 –1494) author of the finely written *Oration on the Dignity of Man,* is even more notable for his optimism, the life affirmation natural to a wealthy, well born young man. He added the Jewish **Kabbala** to the mix.

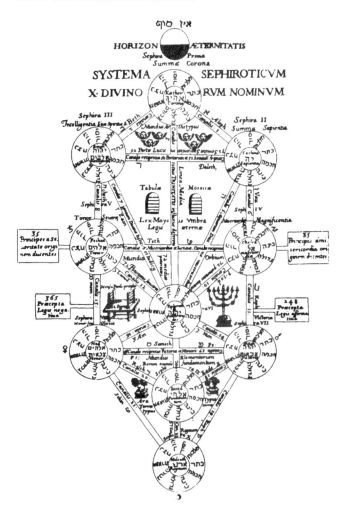

The Tradition

Drier thinkers have accused Pico and Ficino of childishness in their love of mystery. Neoplatonism looks to esoteric mystery as a source of enlightenment. Whatever its intellectual shortcomings, as religion it offers an escape from the dominant ideology of the time. In mystery is a refuge for wisdom.

Ficino's aesthetic impulse was for the unity of nature. He emphasised the scholastic principle that *Natura non facit saltum (Nature doesn't jump)*. At the renaissance neoplatonism took root in several countries including England, where there was a motive to get rid of some old clutter. These ideals survived in art. In Bulwer's time the ideals of the renaissance still managed to shine though.

Neoplatonism brought allegorical interpretations of dogma. The neoplatonic conception of enlightenment emphasised the magical power of ideas and involved the urge to include as many different traditions of wisdom as possible. Renaissance magic developed through Ficino, Pico and Giordano Bruno to influence mainstream philosophy.

Trithemius
1462 –1516

Johannes Trithemius German Benedictine Abbot, was an important link in the chain, teacher of Cornelius Agrippa and Paracelsus. Agrippa called him *"A man very industrious after secret things"*.
In his book *Steganographia* Trithemius ventures further into demonic magic than Ficino had dared, though disguising his book as work of cryptography.

Agrippa
1486 –1535

Heinrich Cornelius Agrippa von Nettesheim, German polymath, produced an encyclopaedic synthesis of the occult tradition as it had been developing, including much mediaeval Jewish material. He was the leading synthetist of Renaissance magic. In Germany he passed into folklore for his great wisdom.

NOW TALL AGRIPPA LIVED CLOSE BY SO TALL, HE ALMOST TOUCHED THE SKY.

The Tradition

Agrippa was a crucial influence on **Bruno** and **Dee**. *JUDICIOUS READER: This is true and sublime Occult Philosophy. To understand the mysterious influences of the intellectual world upon the celestial, and of both upon the terrestrial; and to know how to dispose and fit ourselves so as to be capable of receiving the superior operations of these worlds, whereby we may be enabled to operate wonderful things by a natural power—to discover the secret counsels of men, to increase riches, to overcome enemies, to procure the favor of men, to expel diseases, to preserve health, to prolong life, to renew youth, to foretell future events, to see and know things done many miles off, and such like as these. These things may seem incredible, yet read but the ensuing treatise and thou shalt see the possibility confirmed both by reason and example.* —**John French**, the translator of the English edition of 1651.

As a typical magus he was involved in political intrigue, being sent by the Emperor on a mission to Catalonia to deal with some consequences of a peasant revolt. He was besieged in a tower for several weeks and only escaped by a clever stratagem...

Agrippa, Henry Cornelius. Fourth Book of Occult Philosophy and Geomancy. Magical Elements of Peter de Abano. Astronomical Geomancy: The Nature of Spirits; And Arbatel of Magic.

(Actually this fourth book, which deals with evil spirits, is held to be spurious- a case of pseudepigraphy).

The Tradition

Paracelsus
1493 - 1541

The dominant philosophical strain in the western occult tradition is neoplatonism. Infusing the crude magic of the mediaeval texts with this intellectual philosophy, scholars of the west European renaissance created a sophisticated magus ideal. Renaissance magic developed through Ficino, Pico and Giordano Bruno to influence a major philosopher like **Leibniz**, a vital influence on **Kant**.

Some men who claimed to embody it, like Paracelsus, combined original wisdom with a strong measure of charlatanry. Paracelsus contributed to several branches of science. He is accounted the father of pharmaceutical medicine as well as a great occultist venerated by the Rosicrucians.

Immanuel Kant

THE ALCHEMIST IS HE WHO HELPS TO DEVELOP TO THE EXTREME LIMITS INTENDED BY NATURE THAT WHICH NATURE PRODUCES FOR THE BENEFIT OF MANKIND.

Paracelsus' scientific practice was to accept any story, however bizarre, and seek an explanation for it, that is making the explanation fit the story rather than vice versa.

The Tradition

From *The Haunted and the Haunters:*-

"Let me illustrate what I mean from an experiment which Paracelsus describes as not difficult, and which the author of the Curiosities of Literature cites as credible: A flower perishes; you burn it. Whatever were the elements of that flower while it lived are gone, dispersed, you know not whither; you can never discover nor re-collect them. But you can, by chemistry, out of the burnt dust of that flower, raise a spectrum of the flower, just as it seemed in life. It may be the same with the human being. The soul has so much escaped you as the essence or elements of the flower. Still you may make a spectrum of it. And this phantom, though in the popular superstition it is held to be the soul of the departed, must not be confounded with the true soul; it is but the eidolon of the dead form."

Like **Robert Fludd**, Paracelsus claimed to be a virgin. What did he mean by this? One presumes he did something with his sexual energies other than merely suppressing them. On the other hand there is a legend that he was castrated as a child.

THERE ARE MANY WORLDS: AND WE ARE NOT THE ONLY BEINGS IN OUR OWN WORLD... WE ARE NOT THE ONLY BEINGS MADE; THERE WERE MANY MORE WHOM WE DO NOT KNOW.

Paracelsus believed that each act of masturbation created spiritual beings. His famous account of his manufacture of a homunculus appears to show the element of fraudulence in his character. He claimed he

The Tradition

had successfully created this artificial human being but that it refused to obey him and ran away.

He also purported to possess the elixir of life. This is doubtful, as he died aged only thirty seven. In his defence, it is said he was a great drunkard and his early demise may have been related to that.

His tone was often scornful and sarcastic, one feature about his character that appealed to Nietzsche, who before he settled on the Persian prophet Zarathustra as his mouthpiece had thought of choosing this strikingly original genius.

Friedrich Nietszche

Germany

Bulwer's rejection of Bentham's egoism signals the onset of Victorianism. The characteristic enlightenment of the Georgian era was over and there was a return to more familiarly Christian conceptions of the moral life, where people act morally for the sake of morality, guided by conscience. The influence of Prussia combined with the raw Christianity of Protestant dissenters, who were getting more of a voice in public life. Henceforth we were to be ruled by morality rather than self interest and the workings of the invisible hand. Bentham would not have seen this as progress or accepted that he had overlooked anything.

But for now Germany had much to offer. "*Close thy Byron open thy Goethe!*" urged **Carlyle**. For many Victorians Germany was a romantic repository and an alternative England. Bulwer's England was a vital part of Europe, sharing a common project. Two world wars changed that. After 1945 many continental intellectuals, fearing certain lines of thought, retreated into a bland rationalism. Already distanced from Germany, the British could feel apart from this. Identifying themselves as victors, they did not have to fear their own strength. Instead they had a great despot in the form of American democracy, that they could complain about without too much danger. Bulwer would not have viewed the prospect with much enthusiasm.

In recent times he has been far more popular in Germany than in his home country. Composer Richard Wagner enthusiastically devoured several Bulwer Lytton novels while he was living in Riga, in Latvia. He became an ardent fan and tried to meet him at the House of Commons when he came to England. The influence Bulwer had on him extended way beyond giving him the idea for his opera *Rienzi*. Wagner was trying to do the same kind of thing for Germany he thought Bulwer was doing for England.

Germany

Richard Wagner

Like the self appointed hierophants of the later nineteenth century, Eliphas Lévi, and **Joseph (the Sar) Peladan**, Wagner was a key influence on the artistic movement known as symbolism. He himself built a reputation for great depth and wisdom, which hostile critics would denounce as illusion. He saw himself as magician, as a sort of Klingsor with balls.

The power of Wagner's magic was shown by his genius at emotional manipulation. If yielding to the full enjoyment of his art is a religious experience, the master's ability to arouse and direct such emotion is magic, and a higher order of being.

Its ultimate object can be expressed in symbolic terms as the holy grail or the philosopher's stone, the extraction of maximum satisfaction from life as lived.

According to some critics the yearning that is sung about in *Tristan* suggests a promise of ecstasy never quite completed and which could only be fulfilled in death.

Notoriously Wagner proposed an artistic and cultural programme which had some sinister political implications. Yet understanding him as magician, as seducer, even the excesses of his nationalism can be a path to valuable psychological truths.

Wagner is counted as central to the German soul even today, with its continuing need for redemption. What this might suggest is that the German soul is something created, ruled by magic. Wagner was a magician, as Nietzsche said he was, and Crowley would have approved.

Wagner's operas are full of magic. In *Parsifal* he presents his idea of a villain, Klingsor, a sorcerer who has castrated himself. To Nietzsche, who knew him intimately, Wagner was himself a magician, of a not always benign type.

AH THIS OLD MAGICIAN, HOW MUCH HE IMPOSED UPON US!

Rosicrucians

Bulwer is said to have dropped hints that he was himself an initiate of this mystic brotherhood.

One reason for scepticism is that the Rosicrucians were meant to be superior beings possessed of superhuman powers.

They speak of all mankind as infinitely beneath them; their pride is beyond idea, although they are most humble and quiet in exterior. They glory in poverty, and declare that it is the state ordered for them; and this though they boast universal riches. They decline all human affections, or submit to them as advisable escapes only--appearance of loving obligations, which are assumed for convenient acceptance, or for passing in a world which is composed of them, or of their supposal. They mingle most gracefully in the society of women, with hearts wholly incapable of softness in this direction; while they criticize them with pity or contempt in their own minds as altogether another order of beings from men, (Jennings)

Rosicrucians are central to the western occult tradition as it developed over the centuries. They were a legendary secret society of initiated sages allegedly founded by **Christian Rosencreuz** in 1407. Two hundred years after this date, two manifestos were published announcing a general reform of civilisation and culture on a basis of esoteric wisdom.

They created a stir, with what may have originally been a joke, or at least a prank. Many occultists believe the society really existed and still does as a wise and benevolent force behind history.

Rosicrucianism had a seminal influence on Freemasonry, and of course the Golden Dawn.

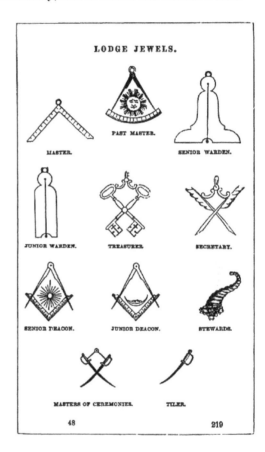

Bulwer Lytton's *Zanoni* is subtitled *A Rosicrucian Tale.*

With its symbolism of the Rose and the Cross, Rosicrucianism is taken to be the leading school of esoteric Christianity, deliberately deceptive as the story

Rosicrucians

of its origins presumably is. Christian Rosencreuz presumably never existed.

An idea hotly resisted by exoteric thinkers is that our society was, should be or even is ruled by elites of sages, the thought behind the Rosicrucian enlightenment. From these mysteries come ideas like government by secret society, which influenced conspiratorially minded Freemasons and Illuminati. True wisdom is only for the initiated. It is not held that enlightenment, in the nature of things, is for the many; if it were offered it would be rejected. But we are to resist the snobbish insinuation that all fulfilment lies with what is openly and officially honoured within society. We must learn to write on more than one level, and to keep these separate. Repudiating the attempt to control the people by officially sponsored mass religion, the Rosicrucian sages recognise the value of popular ideas as bases for popular life. The people need ideas as much as the elite.

We misjudge the renaissance magi if we treat them purely intellectually as philosophers. The esoteric tradition aims at illuminations, states of mind in which spiritual conflicts are resolved. What is sought is not faith but the power bestowed by an adequate symbolism. Through the manipulation of symbols linguistic, kabbalistic, and mathematical we reach towards the form of pure certainty. If some of the precepts sound trite it must be remembered they are mostly detached from dogmatic creeds.

Esoteric philosophy is not like a scientific or philosophical theory, it is more like a map. Thus even the argumentative nature of some of it is not necessarily what it seems to be. This philosophy is beyond all theory. Where there is argument that may be a part of its maplikeness and the only proper question to ask is whether it is a good map or a bad one, not whether it is true or false.

We can see why there is the need for all this to remain hidden. Not only is it so easy for it to be profaned, but the cryptic style of expressing it conveys very much more than otherwise might be said.

The Rosicrucians had a teaching about spirits, which had some influence literary and otherwise.

According to these gentlemen, the four elements are inhabited by spirits which they call Sylphs, Gnomes, Nymphs, and Salamanders. The Gnomes, or demons of earth, delight in mischief; but the Sylphs, whose habitation is in the air, are the best- conditioned creatures imaginable; for they say, any mortal may enjoy the most intimate familiarities with these gentle spirits, upon a condition very easy to all true adepts an inviolate preservation of chastity. (Alexander Pope)

Hargrave Jennings
1817-1890

The explorations of the Rosicrucians may be said to be "as keys to masked doors in the ramparts of nature, which no mortal can pass through without rousing dread sentries never seen upon this side" (A Strange Story)

When Hargrave Jennings published his book *The Rosicrucians their Rites and Mysteries* in 1870 he was accused of both bad writing and pornography. One critic wrote of a '*most unwholesome current*' running through his book. There was some guilt by association with **Edward Sellon**, who had similar ideas as well as a sideline in pornography. Nonetheless Jennings had great influence on many nineteenth century occultists. Bulwer Lytton was a personal friend.

...NO BETTER BOOK UPON SUCH A THEME HAS BEEN WRITTEN, OR INDEED COULD BE WRITTEN UNLESS A MEMBER OF THE FRATERNITY WERE TO BREAK THE VOW WHICH ENJOINS HIM TO SECRECY...

Readers may be reminded of **Freud's** theories, with much of the plausibility of the later movement.

Particularly fascinating is his sexual interpretation of the whole grail legend.

Such ideas would be further developed. Mme Blavatsky would complain about a later version.

...THE SHOWER OF PHALLICISM THAT BURST UPON THE READING PUBLIC IN THE SHAPE OF GENERAL FORLONG'S **RIVERS OF LIFE**. (LUCIFER, JULY, 1896)

Jennings is a much maligned writer, yet arguably a profound one. He was a seer of symbols, like Freud and Jung, but he read them into the environment, thus detecting secret, subversive meanings everywhere. This can be one of the symptoms of madness, but if disciplined it can represent a radically original way of looking at the world, an exciting erotic mode of experiencing the works of civilisation.

Sexualising all its symbolism, he understands Christianity as a fertility religion. The inner significance of this is essentially the defeat of the moralising interpretation. There is no intention of

Hargrave Jennings
1817-1890

reducing faith to sexual activity. A fascinating new field of esoteric religion opens up. The cryptic style of expressing it, conveys very much more than would otherwise be possible.

Through the symbolism of religious history, heraldry, art and legend, and with a wealth of anecdotes, Jennings explores the thesis of an alternative wisdom. He points to the parallels in Hinduism, Buddhism and ancient paganism. He relates the image of the fleur-de-lis to the lotus of Ancient Egypt, there, as in India, a symbols of the female sex organs. He shows how the Arthurian legends are as full of double entendres as the *Roman de la Rose*. He gives an esoteric reading of the knights of the round table.

Concerning the Order of the Garter ceremonies he writes on page 323:-

There are 13 Lunations in the Year, or the Solar Circle: — twice 13 are Twenty-Six, the dark and the light renewals or changes of the Moon (which is feminine). The dark infer the red rose, the light imply the white rose ; both equally noble and coequal in rank with parallel, but different, Rosicrucian meanings. These mythic discs, or red and white roses, correspond with the Twenty-Six Seats, or "Stalls," around the "Round Table" (which is an Apotheosis), allowing two chief seats (or one "Throne") as pre-eminent for the King-Priest, Priest-King, in the "Siege-Perilous." The whole refers to King Arthur and his Knights of the Round Table, set round as sentinels ("in lodge") of the Sangreal, or Holy Graal — the "Sacrifice Mysterious," or "Eucharist." That the Order of the Garter is feminine, and that its origin is an apotheosis of the "Rose," and of a certain singular physiological fact connected with woman's life, is proven in many ways — such as the double garters, red and white; the twenty-six knights, representing the double thirteen lunations in the year, or their twentysix mythic "dark and light" changes of "night and day." "But how is all this magic and sacred in the estimate of the Rosicrucians?" an inquirer will very naturally ask. The answer to all this is very ample and satisfactory; but particulars must be left to the sagacity of the querist himself, because propriety does not admit of explanation. Suffice it to say, that it is one of the most curious and wonderful subjects which has occupied the attention of antiquaries. That archaeological puzzle, the "Round Table of King Arthur," is a perfect display of this whole subject. of the origin of the "Garter;" it springs directly from it, being the same object as that enclosed by the myt/hic garter, "garder," or "girther."

Hargrave Jennings

1817-1890

He was very familiar with Bulwer's work. Bulwer's receptivity to phallicism is indicated by the suggestive phallic sculptures with which he covered the exterior of Knebworth. English Heritage, mindful of the effect on child visitors and their parents, raised no objection to their removal only a few years ago.

Some modern critics follow Blavatsky's dismissal of Jennings, not seeing the mysticism for the sex, unresponsive to its liberating appeal. As with Indian tantrism, much of the mystical effect comes from the taboo breaking quality of the writing. As a pornographer Sellon would have been attuned to this aspect. Postmodernist rhetoric about transgression, and the emancipating promise of Freud's subversive sexuality, are like fragments torn from the occult tradition.

Wagner's Parsifal was premiered in 1884. Did he know Jennings' interpretation of the grail legend?

Eliphas Lévi

1810-1875

"Magic was the science of Abraham and Orpheus, of Confucius and Zoroaster and it was magical doctrines which were graven on tables of stone by Enoch and by Trismegistus. Moses purified and re-veiled them- this being the sense of the word reveal". (Eliphas Lévi)

Some have said Bulwer was a pupil of Lévi. Others that it was the other way round. Lévi had great respect for Bulwer's esoteric knowledge and allegedly deferred to it.

Born in Paris, in 1810 Alphonse Louis Constant changed his name to the exotic sounding Eliphas Lévi. Trained as a priest, he served three prison sentences for inflammatory revolutionary publications.

Eliphas Lévi

He synthesised occultism for a nineteenth century public, laying the ground for the magical revival. His romantic popularisation bestowed a new dimension on the magical tradition. Magic as an esoteric pursuit on the farthermost fringes of the official creed, is a different proposition from magic publicly upheld as a mainstream contribution to the culture of the day. To his English translator, **A E Waite**, Lévi is a sceptic. Waite's idea of the occult seemed to require belief in an objective hierarchy of spirits, with whom we make contact. He quotes St Paul on faith. The fundamental principle of magic is to do with will. In comparison Waite's idea of faith is primitive. He says faith is the *sine qua non* of experience. On the level of experience he is talking about, faith and doubt are the same. The magician is not bound by the demands of metaphysical consistency. To the metaphysical innocent this makes him appear a sceptic and atheist. A mere sceptic would write differently. A profound magical philosophy must include scepticism. Belief and doubt must be compatible. The consistency with one's earthly philosophy may be tenuous. One thing that seems to be relevant is that the earthly philosophy should not deny the possibility of occult experience altogether. Logically it might, but it would be strange.

As soon as he saw my enthusiasm for any idea he led me to consider the opposite idea, thus producing equilibrium. Equilibrium was his aim to such a degree that I sometimes revolted against apparent contradictions. **(Louise Hutchinson, Lévi's English pupil)**

Eliphas Lévi

1810-1875

THE ROMAN DE LA ROSE AND THE DIVINE COMEDY ARE TWO OPPOSITE FORMS OF THE SAME WORK- INITIATION INTO INTELLECTUAL INDEPENDENCE, SATIRE ON ALL CONTEMPORARY INSTITUTIONS AND ALLEGORICAL FORMULATIONS OF THE GREAT SECRETS OF THE ROSICRUCIAN SOCIETY.

In his later work, Lévi insists on his Catholicism, and writes of magic as a forbidden science. There is a natural progression from his form of Catholicism to decadent romanticism. What he makes forbidden is what he has tempted us with as most exotically fascinating. The appeal to man's passions is only intensified by prohibition. The Buddhists knew that what is to be desired must not be forbidden. Yet how is the occult to be enjoyed if it is inextricably bound up with the threat of Hell? By masochism and decadence.

By making his hidden wisdom forbidden, Lévi is a decadent. He opens up an exciting new world which he says we may not enter on pain of damnation, knowing full well that we will.

Some of Lévi's ideas were highly creative and original. For him:

This is an intriguing slant on Dante, and curiously turns the poem *Roman de la Rose*, an unmistakable mediaeval allegory about seduction and sex, into a coded description of something else, namely the highest esoteric wisdom.

Lévi's connection with Bulwer is part of the legend of both men for which it little matters that its intimacy has been disputed. They complement each other. One writer sometimes said to have influenced both is **Francis Barrett**. There was another indisputable one.

"The great thing of the eighteenth century is not the encyclopaedia, not the sneering and derisive philosophy of Voltaire, not the negative metaphysics of Diderot, and D'Alembert, not the malignant philosophy of Rousseau; it is the sympathetic and miraculous physics of **Mesmer**" (E Lévi History of Magic)

Apollonius of Tyana

In his 1856 work *Dogme Et Rituel De La Haute Magie*, parts of which some said he wrote on Bulwer-Lytton's advice, Lévi says he visited the English novelist in London in 1853 and performed, at his request, a magical ritual to evoke the spirit of Apollonius of Tyana.

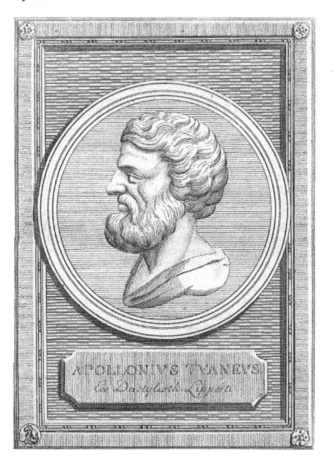

APOLLONIVS TYANEVS

Much of the originality of Greek philosophy lay in capturing in a form acceptable to the rational intellect some of the important insights of religious intuition. The thread runs from the mythical Orpheus,

Orpheus

to the Pythagoreans to Plato, thence though the pagan Neoplatonists, eventually right back into myth with Apollonius of Tyana.

The figure of the miracle working Apollonius was the late pagan answer to the character of the Christian Jesus.

Apollonius of Tyana

There is a life by **Philostratus**, in which Apollonius does not come across as especially interesting or original. Keats portrays him in *Lamia* as a killjoy.

What for the sage, old Apollonius?
Upon her aching forehead be there hung
The leaves of willow and of adder's tongue;
And for the youth, quick, let us strip for him
The thyrsus, that his watching eyes may swim
Into forgetfulness; and, for the sage,
Let spear-grass and the spiteful thistle wage
War on his temples. Do not all charms fly
At the mere touch of cold philosophy?
There was an awful rainbow once in heaven:

We know her woof, her texture; she is given
In the dull catalogue of common things.
Philosophy will clip an Angel's wings,
Conquer all mysteries by rule and line,
Empty the haunted air, and gnomed mine—
Unweave a rainbow, as it erewhile made
The tender-person'd Lamia melt into a shade.

Apollonius' status as a rival to Jesus held not only in the ancient world. Eighteenth century critics of Christianity tried to make something of him as a proponent of a more tolerant universal type of religion, who sought truth all over the world. If what is known of the teaching is bland, much can be imagined of what has been lost.

For Bulwer he was a figure of some significance.

The marvels of Faustus are not comparable to those of Apollonius" (Last Days of Pompeii)

"Yet their knottiest problems have never yet been published. Their sublimest works are in manuscript, and constitute the initiatory learning, not only of the Rosicrucians, but of the nobler brotherhoods I have referred to. More solemn and sublime still is the knowledge to be gleaned from the elder Pythagoreans, and the immortal masterpieces of Apollonius."
"Apollonius, the imposter of Tyanea! are his writings extant?" "Imposter!" cried my host; "Apollonius an imposter!" "I beg your pardon; I did not know he was a friend of yours; and if you vouch for his character, I will believe him to have been a very respectable man, who only spoke the truth when he boasted of his power to be in two places at the same time." "Is that so difficult?" said the old gentleman; "if so, you have never dreamed!" (Ibid)

"Your forefather, who, in the revival of science, sought the secrets of Apollonius and Paracelsus." (Ibid)

Blavatsky

1831-1891

The young Helena Petrovna Blavatsky can be characterised as a Bulwer groupie. Not only is her *Isis Unveiled* full of unacknowledged quotes from Bulwer's novels but she is alleged to have modelled her personality on Madame Liehbur, a character from his *Godolphin*.

JH

In that house, at the time I now speak of, lodged the mysterious Liehbur. It was late at noon, and she sat alone in her apartment, which was darkened so as to exclude the broad and peering sun. There was no trick, nor sign of the fallacious art she professed, visible in the large and melancholy room. One or two books in the German language lay on the table beside which she sat: but they were of the recent poetry, and not of the departed dogmas, of the genius of that tongue.

The enthusiast was alone; and, with her hand supporting her chin, and her eyes fixed on vacancy, she seemed feeding in silence the thoughts that flitted to and fro athwart a brain which had for years lost its certain guide; a deserted mansion, whence the lord had departed, and where spirits not of this common life had taken up their haunted and desolate abode

And never was there a countenance better suited to the character which this singular woman had assumed. Rich, thick, auburn hair was parted loosely over a brow in which the large and full temples would have betrayed to a phrenologist the great preponderance which the dreaming and the imaginative bore over the sterner faculties.

Her eyes were deep, intense, but of the bright and wandering glitter which is so powerful in its effect on the beholder, because it betokens that thought which is not of this daily world and inspires that fear, that sadness, that awe, which few have looked on the face of the insane and not experienced.

Her features were still noble, and of the fair Greek symmetry of the painter's Sibyl; but the cheeks were worn and hollow, and one bright spot alone broke their marble paleness; her lips were, however, full, and yet red, and by their uncertain and varying play, gave frequent glimpses of teeth lustrously white; which, while completing the beauty of her face, aided--with somewhat of a fearful effect--the burning light of her strange eyes, and the vague, mystic expression of her abrupt and unjoyous smile.

Blavatsky

1831-1891

You might see when her features were, as now, in a momentary repose, that her health was broken, and that she was not long sentenced to wander over that world where the soul had already ceased to find its home; but the instant she spoke, her colour deepened, and the brilliant and rapid alternations of her countenance deceived the eye, and concealed the ravages of the worm that preyed within.

The Last Days of Pompeii. From the latter book Arabaces, the high priest of Isis, is credited with first sparking her adventurous career as mystical hierophant. When writing about occultism she cites Bulwer's fictional characters Zanoni and Margrave as readily as the more historical adepts like **Roger Bacon** and the **Comte de St Germain**.

She shifted the centre of occult authority eastwards. She claimed to have travelled to Tibet where she located the Hidden Masters, or Mahatmas, such as *Koot Hoomi* and *Morya,* who instructed her to found the Theosophical Society, which she did in 1875, shortly after Bulwer's death. She kept in contact with them by astral means. Other Theosophists testified to the existence of these adepts, claiming to have communicated and even had physical contact with them.

These *Hidden Masters* of the *Great White Brotherhood*, were obviously similar to the advanced adepts of the Rosicrucian tradition. They reappeared as the Secret Chiefs of the Golden Dawn.

Mme Blavatsky's theosophy was a form of religion. Understanding art as the deliberate creation of significant form, religion is an extension of art. Philosophical ideas are different from theosophical ones, which are often regarded as crude and theosophists as gullible. This is unfair. Theosophy was a programme for religious reform and can be compared with the Rosicrucian manifestos.

Blavatsky

1831-1891

Leaving aside questions as to the reality of Hidden Masters like Koot Hoomi, and Morya, Blavatsky's impulse offered a mythology as serviceable as many others, and provided a stimulating basis for scholars of comparative religion. Theosophists could contribute to this subject every bit as well as orthodox Christians, who have managed to retain respectability up to the present day.

The Mahatma Koot Hoomi

It is quite true that the origin of every religion is based on the dual powers, male and female, of abstract Nature, but these in their turn were the radiations or emanations of the sexless, infinite, absolute Principle,

*the only One to be worshipped in spirit and not with rites; whose immutable laws no words of prayer or propitiation can change, and whose sunny or shadowy, beneficent or maleficent influence, grace or curse, under the form of Karma, can be determined only by the actions--not by the empty supplications--of the devotee. This was the religion, the One Faith of the whole of primitive humanity, and was that of the "Sons of God," the B'ne Elohim of old. This faith assured to its followers the full possession of transcendental psychic powers, of the truly divine magic. (*H P Blavatsky- Buddhism, Christianity and Phallicism*)*

The Theosophist is one who lifts the veils. *Isis Unveiled* is a well chosen title for Blavatsky's book. Thus it is open to us free thinkers to enjoy churches. For all they shout about their own truth claims, all that is merely necessary.

Blavatsky moved the headquarters of the Theosophical society to Adyar, near Madras, in India.

Reading about Blavatsky and her movement is a good antidote to conventional views of the Victorians as solidly Christian. This was much more fun. We can see the value of Theosophy in breaking out of Christianity and building a bridge to the orient.

Religion

By the 1840s Bulwer was talking more about freedom. For him English ideas of freedom were bound up with Protestantism. In *Harold* he shows that the Norman Conquest was sanctioned by the Pope as a proto-crusade, arguing that this brought about a lasting sense of resentment against the papacy. He traces roots of English ideas of freedom in anti-French feeling and the constant need to resist France.

Despite his generally Protestant sympathies, he was wary of the excesses of religious enthusiasts like the Methodists. He deplores how **Wesley** advocated flogging children to *"break their spirit"*.

And yet:-

To the sentiments of Luther the mind of modern Europe is indebted for the noblest revolution it has known.

In 1862 Bulwer writes in a letter to his son:

I accept the Church to which I belong because I think it immaterial to me here and hereafter whether some of its tenets are illogical or unsound, :and because, before I -could decide that question, I must wade thro' an immense mass of learning for which I have no time, and then go thro' .a process of reasoning, for which I have no talent. And when I have ·~ ·done all this, cui bono? . . . It is not my metier.

Yet he says:-

That R.C. faith, between you and me, does produce very fine specimens of adorned humanity-at once so sweet and so heroical. I suspect the Brahminical faith does the same.

Religion

Note that he counts the Roman Catholic faith as a different religion from his own Anglicanism.

Was he even Christian? Though his epic poem King Arthur has a leading theme of the conversion to Christianity, it is a mistake to see him as altogether orthodox. His Christianity is of an esoteric variety, open to the suggestion that all religions are one. Flexible and eclectic, it was little different from theosophy.

Faustus

Agrippa, Dee, Barrett and other exponents of the magical tradition all go to some lengths to explain that their magic is not about making a pact with the Devil.

Glanvill on Witches 1531

Glanvill's book on witches brings ingenious arguments in support of his thesis that diabolic pacts really took place and that witches were guilty of the crimes for which they were executed. He argues against a scepticism which would make "*wise judges*" into murderers.

According to him people did sell their souls to the Devil. That was what Marlowe's Dr Faustus did.

To the esoteric philosopher, the character Faustus was not a magician at all but a precise parable of the ordinary ambitious man.

Marlowe's *Doctor Faustus* is the original classic. Faustus is a foolish magician who makes a bad bargain. But on other interpretations he is being punished for sin, pride, ambition, malice and the overactive will. In this case his punishment is inflicted by a tyrannical God, the same who cursed Adam for eating from the tree of he knowledge of good and evil.

Faustus

Goethe modified the theology.

THE MARVELS OF FAUSTUS ARE NOT COMPARABLE TO THOSE OF APOLLONIUS.

JH

Bulwer was a great admirer of Goethe, and translated him, but his Faust was not his idea of a magician. On Goethe's interpretation the real drama of Faust's life comes down to lot of old alchemy. What is the depth behind all the alchemical symbolism?

...THE GENERATION THAT IS YET STUDYING THE ENIGMAS OF GOETHE'S FAUST.

JH

It can seem quite arbitrary. If there is a clear esoteric meaning, such as we can find in the grail symbolism, it is hard to perceive it. Goethe sets himself up as a religious prophet, but Faust himself does not rise to the level of being a lawgiver. He is a child having a romp.

Goethe is usually supposed to have been writing a drama, even a tragedy, when what he actually wrote was really an alchemical mystery play. Faust was indeed just a tourist, he plays at being a magician, but the benevolent deity is what is really objectionable. It is a purely imaginary construct with no basis even in psychological reality, nothing but an invention. It would be congenial to dictatorial regimes. Indeed when denouncing the cult of **Kafka** the communist East German authorities used to urge Faust as an alternative role model.

Goethe's poem is a confusing attempt to replace Christianity by humanism. It is not an esoteric parable. Goethe changed the point of the story. His Faust is not a mage, he is Everyman, looked over by a benevolent deity who gives him permission to do what he does. He is not even aware of this deity. This is outright theism. Goethe is creating a new conception of God, albeit a more humane one than had existed hitherto. That is to say he is legislating cultural values for a future society. This presages and parallels **Hegel**.

JH

Theosophy

Theosophy may be understood as a replacement for Christianity or alternatively as an esoteric understanding of it. The term long predates Blavatsky, but it came to be identified with the movement she founded. By the end of the nineteenth century her theosophy was something to be taken seriously, like socialism, which was and still is. These days it may be regarded with intellectual derision or even political suspicion, but there is no real reason to see it as false philosophy, any more than socialism is. It is not in itself philosophy, but it can be treated, or approached by it. Yet some philosophy may threaten to undermine religion, even the theosophical kind of religion promoted by **Aldous Huxley** and furthered by **Timothy Leary**.

As with the Rosicrucian manifestos, we can interpret Theosophy in terms of some serious enough projects. Though Renaissance Neoplatonism is not usually regarded as top rank philosophy, that did not stop it appearing wise. Theosophy places emphasis on individual perfection, on the form of wisdom. By a kind of symbolistic shorthand it achieves some of the aims that are sought from complex metaphysics.

Theosophy is about fun things to think, a do-it-yourself religion, whose roots go back to Bulwer-Lytton and *Zanoni*, and beyond that, of course, to the canon of occult literature that Bulwer assimilated.

Insofar as theosophy aims towards the most desirable, in the context of various fanciful cosmologies, imaginary wisdoms, structures of the universe and pedigrees of wisdom, it recalls the atmosphere in which the ancient world moved to Christianity. In the imaginative atmosphere of the first three centuries of the Roman Empire men like **Plutarch** could speculate freely about numerous foreign religious myths and ideas. For others the Jewish tradition offered all kinds of short cuts.

The teachings of the Theosophical Society had a commendable influence on the visual arts. The art of Dutch painter **Mondrian** was originally inspired by a mixture of Theosophy and Goethe's colour theory.

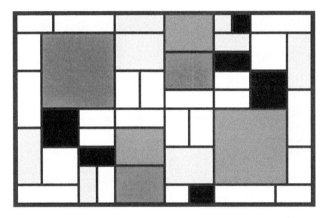

Another Theosophist was **Kandinsky**, who also became a pioneer of abstraction.

Yet another painter, translator of the *Cloud in the Sanctuary,* the theosophist **Isabelle de Steiger**, (1836 – 1927) is interesting for what she illuminates

Theosophy

about a time when theosophy was taken seriously and a form of hierarchical mysticism aroused enthusiasm later ages would put into equality. The hierarchy did not need to be headed by Platonic philosopher kings; much valuable thought flourished below the level of what counts as intellectually respectable. We can be guided by great artists.

Darwin wrote not long before Nietzsche proclaimed that '*God is dead*'. Blavatsky herself was not keen on the God of monotheism. There were alternatives. Oriental religions were becoming ever more familiar. Religious emotion can be employed to liberate from oppressive orthodoxy. Theosophy as Gnosticism frees us from the power of old Nobodaddy the demiurge.

For a modern spirituality some kind of theosophy can be very congenial. It can be quite undogmatic, recognising that surrounding the central ideas teachings and scriptures of the major religions there is something worth understanding. Launch yourself into this study and you may lose the need for dogmatic faith.

In India, notwithstanding Blavatsky's aversion to miscegenation, there arose the idea of a spiritual merger of west and east, of Christianity with Hinduism. With **Annie Besant**, Blavatsky's successor as leader of the Society, it dabbled in religious subversion. The authorities came to see the Theosophical Society as a threat both to British rule in India and the Church of England.

Under Besant and her associate, ex-anglican priest **Charles Leadbeater**, the Theosophists became involved with Indian nationalism. Bulwer has said in *Harold* that every Englishman must support Harold in his fight against the Normans. There is a contradiction between such sentiments and empire. Educate Indians with British culture and nationalism was inevitable.

THEN OLD NOBODADDY ALOFT
FARTED AND BELCHED AND COUGHED,
AND SAID, I LOVE HANGING AND DRAWING AND QUARTERING
EVERY BIT AS WELL AS WAR AND SLAUGHTERING.

Theosophy

There was a fun character to the movement that tended to get forgotten in the seriousness of the postcolonial world, with all the touchiness about national myths. Beyond the idea of a common esoteric wisdom behind and within all religions there were some specific doctrinal innovations, like Leadbeater's books on astral light, thought forms and the chakras.

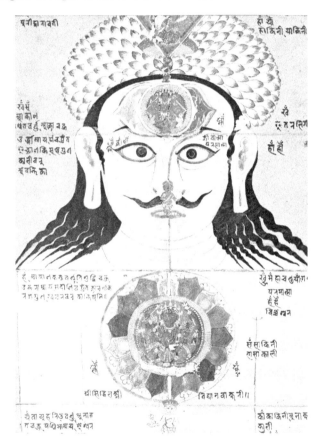

These can fit well together. More controversial was his and Besant's setting up **Krishnamurti** as the new Christ. Many however were prepared to accept the validity of such new religious myths. Bulwer's granddaughter **Emily Lutyens** became much involved with Theosophy and the cult of Krishnamurti.

A R Orage, the English modernist critic for whom Bulwer anticipated Nietzsche, ended his career as a follower of Gurdjieff. **George Gurdjieff**, like Blavatsky was something of a fraud, but interesting and original philosophically and theologically.

A less institutional form of theosophy was carried far into the twentieth century by writers like Christopher Isherwood and Aldous Huxley who proclaimed *the perennial philosophy*. Later Huxley linked such ideas with his experiences under mescalin. A pundit and populariser, he had a significant effect on the spiritual consciousness of his age.

Modern theosophy has educational impact on the mind of the young person. By the mid twentieth century there were many different forces bearing on his spiritual development, all kinds of popular books to attract his attention, and Christianity was not the main theme. How should the churches respond? Could Christians write such books to impress adolescents, they being the future?

Theosophy

In the background there is an aspiration that the new theosophy should take over the existing institutions, even the churches. It was not that the Church of England had lost all its point. Its very wishy-washiness was its real strength. In the 1960s **Michael Ramsey**, Archbishop of Canterbury expressed the view that psychedelic drugs offered a valid route to spiritual experience, and British students of theology were accordingly dropping acid like those from other faculties.

seem silly at the time. They were a form of theosophy, with variations on enlightenment. The poet **Allen Ginsberg** advised him that if he wanted success in America he should abandon the elitism he had leaned from Huxley. He became a mixture of showman, shaman promoting a kind of life affirming anarchy. Following hints from Huxley Leary based his book *The Psychedelic Experience* around the *Tibetan Book of the Dead*.

Of Timothy Leary it is said his psychedelic manuals look "*more than a little silly now*". But they did not

Timothy Leary

Theosophy

Drug religion can be as undogmatic as the shamanism of the nomadic hordes of the steppe, expressing the common theosophy that pervades normal experience. This is inclusive, suited to a late stage in human history.

When we try to understand other religions, like Buddhism or Judaism. To what extent are we ourselves tabooed or excluded? The theosophical is the fellowship that transcends the barriers between religions. Like the Jew who loves Wagner, one wants to feel a fellowship that transcends the barriers people themselves set up.

This may be the main significance of esotericism. Suppose that to my hero, I belong to a class of people who do not deserve to live? It was the idea of the esoteric that allowed communication between Christian, Muslim, pagan, and Jew.

From the mystical point of view no ideas are uniquely true, an idea is as true as its opposite.

There is an academic movement pitting a theory called social construction against Huxley's *perennialism* which is treated as a theory.

To maintain your own vision you need to assert your right to ignore the rights of others and to culturally-appropriate at will, behaving like an intelligent but ignorant barbarian.

THAT YOU HAVE DESPISED, THERE IS MUCH TO HONOUR IN THAT.

We may stick up for our natural misunderstandings on the nature of religious belief. Huxley, Gurdjieff, Blavatsky and Leary offer different routes to a similar goal. It is not mandatory to pursue enlightenment by intellectual understanding.

There are different modes of access to theosophical wisdom. We need to determine the one we want.

Golden Dawn

Arabaces, the villainous Egyptian priest in *The Last days of Pompeii* is the representative of ancient esoteric wisdom. Though Blavatsky began with Egypt, she moved the Theosophical focus further east in the direction of India and Tibet. There were others who stayed with the Egyptians, integrated into esoteric Christianity, keeping to the traditional path taken by occult studies in the west.

Inspired by *Zanoni*, Bulwer's friend **Wynn Westcott** embarked on a course of very serious study. He published a number of well researched books on occult subjects, as well as an erudite one on suicide, drawing on his work as a London coroner. He always believed Bulwer to be an adept initiate. He put his knowledge to use by founding the Hermetic Order of the Golden Dawn. His cofounder **S L "Macgregor" Mathers**, a high grade Freemason, was mainly responsible for devising a set of rituals embodying a body of traditional esoteric wisdom.

S L Mathers

The first temple of the Golden Dawn opened in 1888, 15 years after Bulwer's death. It taught ritual magic, as well as forms of spiritual development that had been covered by Bulwer's reading as well as Levi's exploration of the tradition.

Like the original Rosicrucian society the order's origin story was presumably fictitious. Anna Sprengel was a German aristocrat, now believed to have been invented by Westcott who supposedly ran the order in Germany and licensed the opening of a British temple. Above her were the Secret Chiefs, beings like Blavatsky's Hidden Masters, with whom various leading members would sometimes claim contact while their rivals cried fraud.

As commonly in occult matters there was the problem of establishing authority. Westcott and Mathers needed some for the Golden Dawn. Pseudepigraphy has a recognised place in religious history. Lies may be a legitimate manoeuvre when seeking to establish original ideas. What are the pillars of orthodoxy but lies of another sort? The fountainhead of Christian mysticism, Pseudo-Dionysius, was himself an impostor.

It is surprising how many famous people belonged to the order.

Here is a list of some of them:

Arnold Bennett, novelist (1867-1931)
Algernon Blackwood, occult fiction writer (1869-1951)
Aleister Crowley, occult personality (1875-1947)
Florence Farr, actress (1860-1917)
Dion Fortune, cabbalist (1890-1946)
Maud Gonne, Irish revolutionary (1866-1953)
Annie Horniman, theatre manager (1860-1937)
Arthur Machen, occult fiction writer (1863-1947)
Anna Kingsford, feminist theosophist (1846-1888)

Golden Dawn

Samuel Liddell MacGregor Mathers, occult personality (1854-1918)
Gustav Meyrink, occult novelist (1868-1932)
Israel Regardie, occult writer (1907-1985)
Sax Rohmer, novelist (1883-1959)
Isabelle de Steiger Painter and theosophist (1836–1927)
 Bram Stoker, occult novelist (1847-1912)
Evelyn Underhill, writer on mysticism (1875-1941)
Arthur Edward Waite occult scholar (1857-1942)
William Wynn Westcott, coroner (1848-1925)
Charles Williams, Christian novelist (1886-1945)
William Butler Yeats, poet (1865-1939)

Swedenborg
1688-1772

A Treatise Concerning Heaven and Hell and the Wonderful Things Therein as Heard and Seen by the Honorable and Learned Emanuel Swedenborg.

Emanuel Swedenborg was the son of a Lutheran bishop. After a brilliant career as a scientist, he embarked on a new one as a mystic visionary elaborating a number of traditional occult themes, like conversing with spirits and the hermetic idea of correspondences (*as above so below*), as well as the idea of esoteric reading. In his *Heaven and Hell* he has this to say about the latter place:-

488. *How the delights of everyone's life are changed after death into things that correspond can be known from a knowledge of correspondences; but as that knowledge is not as yet generally known I will try to throw some light on the subject by certain examples from experience. All who are in evil and who have established themselves in falsities in opposition to the truths of the church, especially those that have rejected the Word, flee from the light of heaven and take refuge in caves that appear at their openings to be densely dark, also in clefts of rocks, and there they hide themselves; and this because they have loved falsities and hated truths; for such caves and clefts of rocks,[2] well as darkness, correspond to falsities, as light corresponds to truths. It is their delight to dwell in such places, and undelightful to dwell in the open country.*

[2] Those that have taken delight in insidious and secret plots and in treacherous machinations do the same thing. They are also in such caves; and they frequent rooms so dark that they are even unable to see one another; and they whisper together in the ears in corners. Into this is the delight of their love changed. Those that have devoted themselves to the sciences with no other end than to acquire a reputation for learning, and have not cultivated their rational faculty by their learning, but have taken delight in the things of memory from a pride in such things, love sandy places, which they choose in preference to fields and gardens, because sandy places correspond to such studies.

[3] Those that are skilled in the doctrines of their own and other churches, but have not applied their knowledge to life, choose for themselves rocky places, and dwell among heaps of stones, shunning cultivated places because they dislike them. Those that have

Swedenborg

1688-1772

ascribed all things to nature, as well as those that have ascribed all things to their own prudence, and by various arts have raised themselves to honors and have acquired wealth, in the other life devote themselves to the study of magic arts, which are abuses of Divine order, and find in these the chief delight of life.

[4] Those that have adapted Divine truths to their own loves, and thereby have falsified them, love urinous things because these correspond to the delights of such loves.

[3] Those that have been sordidly avaricious dwell in cells, and love swinish filth and such stenches as are exhaled from undigested food in the stomach.

[5] Those that have spent their life in mere pleasures and have lived delicately and indulged their palate and stomach, loving such things as the highest good that life affords, love in the other life excrementitious things and privies, in which they find their delight, for the reason that such pleasures are spiritual filth. Places that are clean and free from filth they shun, finding them undelightful.

[6] Those that have taken delight in adulteries pass their time in brothels, where all things are vile and filthy; these they love, and chaste homes they shun, falling into a swoon as soon as they enter them. Nothing is more delightful to them than to break up marriages. Those that have cherished a spirit of revenge, and have thereby contracted a savage and cruel nature, love cadaverous substances, and are in hells of that nature; and so on.

Swedenborg's extraordinary account of his cosmic travels reveals considerable power of intellect. His theology is always ingenious. Balzac's mystical novel *Seraphita* is built around his ideas. Lévi was deeply impressed by his system and counted him an occult master worthy of study. Note the condemnation of magic as one of the pastimes of the damned.

Most people may see their lives more as products of fate than deliberate choice. In the Swedenborgian heaven normal life receives a kind of apotheosis as the expression of a virtuous will. It needs the idea of innocence to make it intelligible. One may feel Swedenborg's encomium on the innocence of children comes down to personal idiosyncrasy. Not everyone remembers early childhood as his own innocence or that of others.

Swedenborg
1688-1772

The satisfaction afforded by virtue is but one side of the coin. One will want to turn it over sometimes. William Blake's response in his *Marriage of Heaven and Hell* is much better known than Swedenborg himself:-

I have always found that Angels have the vanity to speak of themselves as the only wise; this they do with a confident insolence sprouting fromF systematic reasoning;Thus Swedenborg boasts that what he writes is new; tho' it is only the Contents or Index of already publish'd books. A man carried a monkey about for a shew, & because he was a little wiser than the monkey, grew vain, and conceiv'd himself as much wiser than seven men. It is so with Swedenborg: he shows the folly of churches and exposes hypocrites, till he imagines that all are religious & himself the single one on earth that ever broke a net. Now hear a plain fact: Swedenborg has not written one new truth: Now hear another: he has written all the old falsehoods. And now hear the reason. He conversed with Angels who are all religious, & conversed not with Devils who all hate religion, for he was incapable thro' his conceited notions. Thus Swedenborg's writings are a recapitulation of all superficial opinions, and an analysis of the more sublime, but no further. Have now another plain fact: Any man of mechanical talents may from the writings of Paracelsus or Jacob Behmen, produce ten thousand volumes of equal value with Swedenborg's and from those of Dante or Shakespeare, an infinite number.

I WAS WALKING AMONG THE FIRES OF HELL, DELIGHTED WITH THE ENJOYMENTS OF GENIUS; WHICH TO ANGELS LOOK LIKE TORMENT AND INSANITY.

Blake's criticism is spot on.

Swedenborg discounts the myth of the fall of the angels All angels and devils were once men, he says. His moralistic selflessness is one type of the religious mentality. He is against all carnal, sensual amd selfish motives. (in their place, for the angels, are neighbour love and love of God, which is higher). Perhaps for most moderns, including Muslims, this is the essence of religion. In opposing it Blake represents an England that by Swedenborg's standard is diabolic.

"The Scandinavian dreamer speaks from celestial heights as the friend, nay, the instructor, of angels, and his hysterical utterances, that reflect the violent climatic changes of his home, are always expected to contain some hidden allegory which his disciples must unravel if they wish to save their souls:" (Norman Douglas)

Swedenborg explains exactly how and why evil brings punishment in Hell. Evil always desires to do malice, and that is only restrained by punishment and its fear. Devils happily hurt each other just because they are so full of malice. They all live in falsities, united in societies like angels. He is firmly Protestant, expressing hostility to papists as embodying all the vices of self love and carnality.

Swedenborg saw self love as what motivates the worst of the devils in hell. The less evil ones are led by love of the senses. The devils defend their falsities against each other. Implicit is the condemnation of the whole eighteenth century psychology insofar as it reduces everything to self love.

Is it fanciful to link up his mentality with modern Sweden and the conformism of its social democratic ideology?

Wisdom of the Chaldeans

"You have reflected deeply, for an Italian," said Glyndon.
"Who told you I was an Italian?"
"Are you not? And yet, when I hear you speak my own language as a native, I..."
"Tush!" interrupted Zanoni, impatiently turning away.

Eventually we gather that originally Zanoni must have been a Chaldean. These were the heirs of the world's oldest literate civilisation, that founded by the Sumerians.

Iamblichus on The Mysteries of the Egyptians Chaldeans and Assyrians, 1821.

It was Psellus and Plethon who were responsible for collecting the Chaldean oracles together from scattered sources in different ancient writers. The Zoroaster of the oracles is not the same as the prophet of Mazdaism, rather he was *a kind of hatstand on which to hang the sayings and doings of a number of people* as Aleister Crowley put it, comparing him to the Jesus of the gospels. Often obscure, mysterious and suggestive, the oracles are a mixture of Greek Neoplatonism and Persian or older material.

The Chaldeans are most famous for early astronomy, the art of raising spirits and for the custom of temple prostitution. Chaldean myth was not highly systematised, but vivid and elemental. It was the raw religious matter out of which both Hellenic and Hebraic culture were formed.

Chaldean, Babylonian, or Assyrian myth includes much of the same material as the Bible, but that has turned it all into moral tale, compressed it all into a message of obedience to a spiritual despot. Previously myth was free to convey even the deepest atheistical ambiguities.

Greek myth after Homer was different again, in its most serious form it was political, deeply involved with the drive to power and organisation. Homer and Aeschylus present problems to tackle, there is a sense of advancing destiny, of history of a polis, of individual uniqueness. Their gods were more human, more personalised, even eroticised.

The characteristic note of the Old Testament, echoing the Chaldean, is a mysterious atmosphere of religious sublimity.

The Bible is our gateway to an older world, where things do not seem so new as they were to the Greeks and Romans, where there are no institutions to create but everything proceeds in a timeless manner.

The easterners' religion was more intensely immanent. To relate to it it we need to read the earlier books of the Bible and simply ignore the final authority of Jehovah.

William Stirling

1861-1902

One modern exponent of the tradition wrote a book that was too obscure for Westcott. Stirling, a Scottish architect, published *The Canon* in 1897. He was a friend of **Wyndham Lewis** when he was a student at the Slade, and of the artist **William Rothenstein**, who painted his portrait, now lost. He was also acquainted with Golden Dawn member W B Yeats. He committed suicide by cutting his own throat.

His book offers an explanation of the esoteric symbolism of religion, which bears interestingly upon art.

"The old artists, who were piously instructed in the Ecclesiastical Tradition, always represented St Helena and the cross according to the mystic sense. That the theoretical treatment was still known in the sixteenth century is attested by one of the most beautiful pictures in the world- that of Paolo Caliari (National Gallery 1041). The artist has depicted the invention as a visionary revelation merely, but he has taken care that the mystery of the true cross is presented with significant accuracy".

On the above interpretation, it is indeed a very beautiful painting.

Stirling explained that rhetoric is the art of saying one thing while seeming to say another, that the real meaning of religion is not morality at all, that morality is only mores, custom.

William Stirling

1861-1902

"Of the morality which the philosophers have attempted to combine without their theological myths, we have said nothing, because very often it is only an irrelevant accessory. ...Morals, of course, are merely customs (mores). Each code is a local and temporal affair, constructed to suit the exigencies of the times and place, and no more states the law finally and absolutely than any one of the extant theologies states the true nature of the deity".

Wisdom of the Egyptians

Plato and other ancient Greeks had immense respect for the wisdom of the Egyptians.

However, historians tell us that by the time the Greeks became aware of it the Egyptian religion had already grown confused and decadent. **Plutarch** and other writers linked the Egyptian gods and their stories to their own Hellenistic mythology.

Like the ancients some modern historians have employed their discoveries in the service of their own religious ideas and values. American historian **J H Breasted** had a widely influential interpretation of Pharaoh Akhenaton as the first monotheist, presenting his reforms as epochal religious progress, as it is understood in the Abrahamic faiths. The view influenced Freud for his essay *Moses and Monotheism*.

Interpretations of the Bible depend much on ideological preconceptions and predispositions. When assessing the authority of the scholar it is a good idea to look at his presuppositions.

How much can one understand the Egyptians, Babylonians and Assyrians? The recovery of ancient history from the nineteenth century onwards enables modern man to mythologise anew.

Deciphering the ancient texts was making great strides in the latter nineteenth century and some interesting new interpretations became possible. Cambridge-trained Egyptologist **Wallis Budge**, Keeper of Assyrian and Egyptian antiquities at the British Museum, around the corner from where the Golden Dawn had its temple, used to assist Florence Farr, and was sympathetic to the Egyptianism of the Golden Dawn. Were they closer to a genuine affinity with that ancient civilisation than anything for thousands of years? Or was it just another modern misreading?

Budge suggests that some kind of moral dualism pervades the religion of all the ancient cultures except Egypt. He attributes this to the African origins of its civilisation. There is an implication that this shows the superiority of the Egyptian for all the apparent obsession with death.

Wisdom of the Egyptians

This raises interesting questions of what Nietzsche called the transvaluation of values.

Some people feel the ancient Egyptian religion reflects more than other faiths the structure of their own minds. Aleister Crowley showed a preference for Egyptian religion. He made use of this first grandly systematic religion, to convey the idea of a procession of aeons. For his purposes the Egyptian scheme was preferable to, for example, that of the Buddhists. If it lacks in philosophy, as religion it has, or seems to have, a minimum of oppressive dogma.

To some it seems the ancient Egyptians really knew something we don't, more about states of mind and their place on a spiritual map, more about such things as the form of the object of all striving, a personal relationship with the forces of nature, an emotionally satisfying understanding of the cosmos. The next stage is Pythagorean efforts to reach the same understanding intellectually.

As the source of alchemy the Egyptian civilisation seemed to have had a close understanding of the Great Work, and what the real point of life is. The sexual nature of the Great Work involves coming to terms with oneself and all one's experience, transmuting what is painful and unsatisfactory. We may imagine Egypt as a culture where such wisdom was encouraged and there is resistance to everything that is against the Great Work, or the alchemical transmutation of one's own life.

Elements from the old religion went into the Hellenistic mix, of which Hermeticism was one product. For the origins of Christianity it is said we should look beyond Judea and consider the ferment of ideas in the wider region, particularly Egypt. Giordano Bruno traced Christianity back to an original Egyptian religion and got burnt at the stake for his pains. Insofar as early Christianity involved to a great extent a reform of Isis worship, he had a sound historical point. **Frances Yates** describes him as a Catholic but not a Christian.

Credulity

How credulous was Bulwer?

Rosicrucians

He claimed to believe in the existence of the Rosicrucian Fraternity.

Magic

I DO BELIEVE IN THE SUBSTANCE OF WHAT IS CALLED MAGIC.

JH

Ghosts

Partly inspired by Swedenborg, the new religion of spiritualism emerged in the USA.

Mr. Emerson , in the last lecture of his recent series at Boston, spoke of the manner in which a great man's thought diffuses itself, and gets respected, in a generation or two, widely and mechanically. After using several other illustrations, he said that the law is strikingly revealed in the midnight fumblings over mahogany throughout the country now, to get at the secrets of the spiritual world. It always happens, he said, that whatever spirit is called up — Franklin , or Fenelo , or Napoleon, or Abd-el-Kadcr—it is always Swedenborg that answers. That is the cow from which all the milk comes. (The Spiritualist 1856)

In 1853 Bulwer listened to some table rapping. Eighty years later **Virginia Woolf** made fun of this episode in *Flush* her spoof biography of Mrs Browning's cocker spaniel.

From England the news came that Sir Edward Bulwer-Lytton had imported "several of the American rapping spirits" to Knebworth, with the happy result — so little Arthur Russell was informed when he beheld a "strange-looking old gentleman in a shabby dressing-gown" staring at him at breakfast — that Sir Edward Bulwer-Lytton believed himself invisible.

Bulwer invited the American medium **D D Home** to Knebworth in 1855. Elsewhere Home had been reported to have levitated out of one window into another. He was also said to have made a grand piano fly through the air.

Bulwer was not as sceptical of Home as Lévi, let alone Browning, who in face of his wife's credulity wrote the acerbic satirical poem *Mr Sludge the "Medium"*.

Fairies

Bulwer was open to belief in psychic phenomena. As far as spiritualism goes, he did not accept that messages came from the dead as was claimed. Like Conan Doyle he accepted the existence of *"brownies or fairies"* and attributed the phenomena to them. By the nineteenth century believing in fairies was odd, if not quite so laughable as today, but 200 years earlier John Aubrey had written of *Fairies, Fairy-Folk* or *brownies* as a normal part of country life.

Credulity

Come Unto These Yellow Sands
Richard Dadd

Aubrey, John. Miscellanies upon Various Subjects, 1784

How much is credulity even essential to the occult? Bulwer was interested in all the subjects that would concern **The Society for Psychic Research**.

Now, my theory is that the Supernatural is the Impossible, and that what is called supernatural is only a something in the laws of nature of which we have been hitherto ignorant. Therefore, if a ghost rise before me, I have not the right to say, "So, then, the supernatural is possible," but rather, "So, then, the apparition of a ghost is, contrary to received opinion, within the laws of nature—i.e. not supernatural." (The Haunted and the Haunters).

On the Continent you will find still magicians who assert that they can raise spirits. Assume for the moment that they assert truly, still the living material form of the magician is present; and he is the material agency by which from some constitutional peculiarities, certain strange phenomena are represented to your natural senses.

Accept again, as truthful, the tales of Spirit Manifestation in America—musical or other sounds—writings on paper, produced by no discernible hand—articles of furniture moved without apparent human agency—or the actual sight and touch of hands, to which no bodies seem to belong—still there must be found the medium or living being, with constitutional peculiarities capable of obtaining these signs. In fine, in all such marvels, supposing even that there is no imposture, there must be a human being like ourselves, by whom, or through whom, the effects presented to human beings are produced.

This of course was in his fiction.

He wrote to Lady Combermere:

I should not come at once to the notion that they were the bad and perilous demons hostile to the human soul which the old monks too rashly derived from passages in Scripture, ignorantly interpreted. There may be intermediate beings of mixed nature, not deliberately evil nor steadily benevolent, — capricious, uncertain, and only able to get at crude and imperfect rapport with humanity. They may amuse themselves with taking feigned names and sporting with mortal credulity, and be delusive and erring prompters or advisers without any settled motive. A Mr. Beaumont about 200 years ago records two visitations that he supposed he had from spirits. They appeared to him in numbers ; they spoke to him and made music ; they haunted him for months. He asked them what they were — they did not answer that.

Hermeticism

Anon (*actually Mary Anne Atwood*) - A Suggestive enquiry into the Hermetic Mystery, and alchemy, 1850.

Written with the assistance and on the advice of her father, the Rev Thomas South this book was published anonymously. On reading it after publication South decided it gave away too many Hermetic secrets, bought up as many copies as he could and burnt them.

Mary's friend, Golden Dawn member Isabelle de Steiger, republished it after her death in 1910.

The inrush of Greek scholars following the collapse of the Byzantine empire, helped stimulate the new spirit of enquiry that was felt in western Europe during the Renaissance. Dissatisfied with the mediaeval synthesis of Catholic dogma and Aristotle's science of qualities, it was now felt that perhaps all mysteries could be made clear to the understanding. One of the forms taken by this movement was an interest in and the writings attributed to Hermes Trismegistus, according to which the understanding of the workings of nature is intimately involved with the individual's quest for perfection.

Before translating the works of Plato which Plethon had brought to Florence, **Cosimo de' Medici** asked Ficino to translate the Hermetic writings ascribed to Hermes Trismegistus, which he had also obtained and wanted to read before he died.

Thrice great Hermes was identified not only as the Greek Hermes, but also with the Egyptian Thoth, Tahuti, the ibis headed god of wisdom.

Hermeticism

Art, magic and science were the key to the secrets of the universe, to learn which was to attain to perfection within it, maximum individual fulfilment, even godhood. At the least, by studying the nature of the cosmos, a man might discover his innermost will, dispensing with the need for blind trust in spiritual authority. There were hermetic memory systems which can also be looked upon as systems for the coordination and focussing of the will. Truth was rational, but not to be acquired by exclusively intellectual methods. The will to perfection was to find its way as much by intuition as by logical demonstration, and would often express itself in obscure, symbolic terminology.

Trismegistus become proverbial for deep secret wisdom.

> *By Bacchus, quoth Panurge, this was a Notable Chapter, a most Authentic Gloss o' my word! Is this all that the Trismegistian Bottle's Word means? i' troth I like it extreamly, it went down like Mother's Milk.*
>
> *Nothing more, return'd Bacbuc, for Trinc is a Panomphean Word, that is, a Word understood, us'd and celebrated by all Nations, and signifies Drink.*

Aristotle provided a set of concepts with which we are to explain and handle our experience; Hermeticism provides a different set and there were moves in the universities to replace the former with the latter. Hermeticism may not have been top drawer philosophy but as an alternative system to Aristotelianism it was very fruitful. It is not to be refuted by logical argument, unless it is misunderstood. It is neither as pedantic as Aristotelianism, nor as dogmatic.

This invigorating attitude was seminal to the genesis of modern science. Grand utopian programmes were conceived on the basis of esoteric wisdom, and Europe buzzed with hope for the future. However, the scholarly dating of the Hermetic writings to the Neoplatonic rather than the Mosaic era, was a dampener. Henceforth the direct connection between macrocosm and microcosm, the truths of nature and the whole will of man, lost much of its authority.

> *In 1614, French born scholar **Isaac Casaubon**, a religious refugee living in England, plausibly dated the hermetic writings to around 200 AD, so undermining the received belief that Trismegistus was a contemporary of Moses. Isaac was the father of the **Meric Casaubon** who published Dee's account of his commerce with spirits. Both father and son thus did much to discredit the occult for the next few generations.*

The movement known as the Enlightenment is usefully seen in relation to the earlier, Hermetic movement, which it superseded. Many of the ideals of the older outlook were retained in a modified form, and helped to give impetus to rationalism as a social and cultural force. There was an important difference though. The enlightenment rationalist would not allow the authority esoteric religion gives to inner experiences. One of the principal developments characterising the thought of the European Enlightenment was the clear separation of the knower from the known, classically expressed in **Descartes'** dualism. Mind and matter were now seen as two entirely independent substances, and the

Hermeticism

material universe was to be explained in purely mechanistic terms.

We are the heirs of more than the eighteenth century Enlightenment and the Christianity that is understood by most historians. However much we admire the Renaissance, we could never reproduce it when we do not understand its mainsprings. There is much in our surroundings that we could appreciate better if we paid sympathetic attention to this chapter in the history of ideas. There is a coherent tradition which we could learn to read, as perhaps Bulwer had taught himself to read it, and which appears to most moderns as mere confusing gobbledegook.

As above so below; the large depends on the small. The identity of macrocosm and microcosm means the solution to my problems is the key to the solution of the world's problems. A modern scholar tries to be content with his own specialised corner of life, if he does not want to be dismissed as a dilettante.

If Hermeticism left the scientific mainstream, it survived for a while in occult and literary circles. The magus aspires to a position close to complete freedom of spirit and insists that full enlightenment is possible. Total philosophical understanding was accessible to him who refuses to constrain himself within the bounds of any one discipline. The seventeenth century "metaphysical mind" has been described as one living amidst several quite contrary and incompatible intellectual and spiritual worlds. This leaves out the role of the Hermetic philosophy in making this diversity intelligible and acceptable. For Henry Vaughan and Thomas Browne, Hermeticism expressed a feeling that within nature there is a spiritual language that can be discovered. If more people could come to share this language, civilisation would be improved.

For the Hermeticist there is a level on which even the wildest desires are satisfiable. No avenue of knowledge may be left unexplored and most complete understanding is ultimately possible. We are not just to take one option out of the whole range of possibilities but must rise to a level where they are all accessible.

From this viewpoint he can hope to see what is wrong with current values and assumptions, analyse what these are, and delineate a remedy. To judge what is wrong in the light of what should be, is to set right what can be set right by thought and understanding. Values and attitudes are the essence of religion. When thought is free it really can underpin reality, which is the real message of Plato, it can create experience itself. 'Matter' in the Gnostic sense becomes the faeces of

Hermeticism

necessity as when the possibility of thought appears bound and restricted by practical considerations to a particular social and cultural framework.

The philosophical rehabilitation of concepts which rational criticism has supposedly exposed as superstition is a common theme throughout history. An example is the response of the compilers of the Hermetic canon, in Hellenistic Egypt, to rationalist criticisms of the "worship of idols", like those advanced by Mohammed somewhat later. The Egyptians were accused of bowing down to graven images of wood and stone, basing their religion on the false idea that their statues have life.

Therefore their whole faith was held to be irrational. In defence, the sophisticated believer denies that he would ever be so foolish as to imagine the statues had souls. The idea of an inner life to statues was quite irrelevant to his religion. He argues that the figures he worships are symbolic representations of the gods, which are themselves symbols of the higher intelligences described in the Platonic philosophy. The Hermeticist declined to accept this position, claiming that it did not reflect what people felt when they worshipped the gods. If they did not think of the statues as possessing souls, worship would be empty and meaningless. Accordingly, some intellectual effort was put into giving them souls. According to the Hermetic treatise *Aesculapius* the Egyptian priests were able to bring down Platonic intelligences by magical means to inhabit their statues, and instructions were given for doing that. This interpretation cannot be said to have exactly restored the views of the ordinary believer. However it was to have mileage in the development of demonic magic from Ficino to Agrippa, Paracelsus and beyond.

Disillusion

Like John Stuart Mill, Tennyson, Dickens and other leading Victorians, Bulwer came to feel doubts about the direction society was taking.

Strong reservations about equality are expressed in Zanoni. Some quotes anticipate Nietzsche, for whom:

INJUSTICE LIES IN THE CLAIM TO EQUAL RIGHTS.

"*A nation that aspires to equality is unfit for freedom. Throughout all creation, from the archangel to the worm, from Olympus to the pebble from the radiant*

and completed planet to the nebula that hardens through ages of mist and slime into the habitable world, the first law of nature is inequality."

Statements like this have led to oversimplified accusations of reaction. Some critics have treated esoteric Christianity as a reactionary political idea as if the call were for religious orthodoxy and conventional morality. This view appears to spring from ignorance. The idea of progress may be quite narrowly conceived.

Lévi too seemed to have abandoned the radicalism of his youth when he declared that liberty, equality and fraternity were an incompatible combination.

LIBERTY AND EQUALITY NECESSARILY CONFLICT, AND THAT STRUGGLE WILL MAKE FRATERNITY IMPOSSIBLE.

Phallicism

The Dilettante society was founded in 1734 by Sir Francis (*Hellfire*) Dashwood as a dining club for gentlemen who had travelled in Italy. Horace Walpole scathingly observed that the real membership qualification was being drunk.

Nevertheless the society did embark on some very serious work, including funding scholarships for the Grand Tour and campaigning for the foundation of the Royal Academy. One of its publications was *Discourse on the Worship of Priapus, Theology of the Ancients*, which came out for strictly limited circulation, in 1780.

The author, Richard Payne Knight (1750-1824) was to become a man of many accomplishments, classical scholar, collector, numismatist, amateur architect, landscape gardener, aesthetician and member of parliament.

The basis of Knight's thesis came from the theories of his friend the Frenchman Pierre François Hugues, who called himself **Baron D'Hancarville**. D'Hancarville wrote a vast and diffuse study, said to be largely unreadable.

On the usual account, Priapus, son of Dionysus and Aphrodite, has a humble place among classical divinities.

Hera, Queen of the gods, disapproving of Aphrodite's adultery with Adonis while her husband was on his expedition to India, cast a spell on her while she was about to give birth. So Priapus was born hideously ugly with a grotesquely enlarged genitals, as a punishment for the immorality of his mother.

He became the ithyphallic god of male virility, used as a scarecrow. According to another story, found in Macrobius, his father was Pan. In fact, argues Knight, Priapus was the original godhead, though in later antiquity his reputation sadly declined.

Phallicism

Knight amplified and developed D'Hancarville's theories. D'Hancarville had argued that the universality of phallic worship argued for a common source. For Knight this religion was the natural product of common and universal experience.

Greek religion connected naturally with the Hindu lingam/yoni worship of which Europeans were becoming aware. There was a universal language of symbols, which can also be read in what we know of the ancient Egyptian religion.

That religion had been comprehensively destroyed by the Persians when Egypt was part of their empire, so we cannot learn its true nature from the accounts that have survived, like those of Herodotus or Manetho. Knight was also far more explicit than his predecessor about including Christianity in his theory. Identifying

Christ himself with Priapus, he interpreted the Cross as a phallus.

He provides his readers with many engravings of such curious and amusing little objects.

He once said he would be happy to count himself a *"good Christian, did I understand the meaning of the term"* in which case we would have to consider his Christianity to have been of an esoteric variety. That would make him a phallus worshiper.

His phallicism offered an alternative to the standard Neoplatonist view of religious symbolism. He makes it plausible in a psychological sense; phallus worship comes across as healthy, understandable and acceptable to thinking people. We might say he shifts the secret from philosophy to psychology, bypassing Plato altogether.

To discover the truth about Greek religion, Knight says we should look at the Orphic hymns, rather than the usual sources like Homer or Hesiod, let alone Ovid. Then we can correctly read the symbols put on coins by

Phallicism

magistrates who were initiates into the mysteries. What we discover is a subversive Eros-based mystery religion. The Orphics, as they are known, did indeed identify Priapus with the fertility principle that, under the name of Bacchus, was central to their worship.

So instead of Ovid and Hesiod, we must study Plutarch, the Orphic fragments, **Apuleius** and **Macrobius**, in order to learn how to read between the lines. Macrobius (active c 430 AD) was an ancient antiquarian, a man much after Knight's stamp, a collector of curious information.

Significantly, Knight believed the God of the Jews and Christians was Himself by origin none other than the supreme principle of the Orphics.

There is a story repeated by many writers to the effect that horrified by the hostile reception Knight suppressed the copies of his *Discourse*. This does not appear to be true but it appealed to the prudish minds of Christian commentators who preferred to ascribe his masterpiece to some deplorable youthful aberration.

At the end of the century some attacks on him were inspired by a clearly reactionary motive. In the years after the French Revolution any hostility to Christianity was considered politically subversive. In 1794 he was fiercely denounced by a high Tory church magazine *The British Critic*.

Shortly afterwards he was viciously satirised by Thomas James Mathias in a scurrilous poem *Pursuits of Literature*, where he was dismissed as producing material for the '*obscene revels of Greek scholars*', conjuring up distasteful images of masturbating professors.

A self-righteous sanctimony has long been one of the elements of English life. We still have to live with the prurience of critics and gutter journalism, and this can act as a foil to our own heretical affirmation. Like the ancient Gnostics, we seek the more complete liberation that comes with overcoming oppression. The joy in that depends to a great extent on the continued existence of that which is to be overcome.

Whatever the shortcomings of the phallicist theories from a historian's viewpoint, they are as seminal and suggestive as much of Freud.

Magic

What is the point of Magic?

Science

Magic is popularly understood as false science, the attempt to produce an effect where a natural connection between the cause and the effect is mistakenly believed to exist. Undoubtedly magic in this sense can work. Belief can itself open up a great range of mental experiences. Identifying what is magic and what is not we avoid getting **mesmerised** by fake science. We perceive the limits of its usefulness as magic.

There are many kinds of magic. It lacks the objectivity of science, its aims are different. Scientific knowledge can be formalised, magical knowledge is subjective, closely related to desire and usually not universalisable. Pseudoscientific ideas that are interesting but to which we should not yield out minds may be classified as magic. In our culture Marxian and Freudian elements can have the attraction and emotional charge of magic Pseudoscience, which inspires the credulous, is often a means of reacting to sets of phenomena as much as or rather than scientific theories.

It is customary to assert that magic is mistaken science, but that does not do it justice. Pure science is disinterested enquiry, applied science or technology is the provision of means to ends. Magic is concerned with the satisfaction of desire.

Religion

As the means taken to procure satisfaction of desire magical technique can come to provide a polar alternative to religion. In general it can be said that religion is a system for the regulation, direction and control of desire, therefore the outlook underlying magical practice is unamenable to religious constraint.

Magic

By the standards of religious people, magic is actively immoral, but magical knowledge is also useful knowledge. It is useful to know speedy ways to the accomplishment of one's desires. By its nature magical knowledge cannot be common.

On a broader understanding of the term "*religion*" it need not conflict even with individualistic magic. Nevertheless, this concept of magic subverts orthodox faith. From its viewpoint the only justification for accepting orthodox religion is laziness and conformity. What appears to the orthodox as a monstrous lack of religion, is only a different form of religion. The magical philosopher could take on the role of a singularly non repressive kind of priest. Magic by itself can provide the ritual and formulae one loses by rejecting a common church. The magician is the true religious individualist, the ultra Protestant.

Culture

Where there is a formal ritualised method of bringing about some state of mind the connection between the ritual and the desired state is not fixed in nature. Much art and culture may be thought of as systems of magic, the zeitgeist itself as a magical aura or medium. Through persuasion it is possible to effect change, to overcome much of the resistance with which we are faced and to experience a consequent delight.

Individualism

The individualist magician cultivates an internal aesthetic, caring little what people think of him. There is an almost deliberate embrace of what may look like failure, an ultra individual selfish concern. Many magical tablets have survived from the ancient world, notably those consisting of curses. Cursing is described as a "*nasty schizoid type of aggression*".

Magic explores odd whims of the will, like opium fancies, possibilities barely considered in mainstream culture.

Magic

Magic and art

All original art is akin to madness. On virgin paths one is on one's own; the multitude decry. As one moves into the unaccounted, one is doing something of which sane conventional wisdom has always denied the validity. Sanity is judged by the experience of the multitude, and even by its most liberal formulae that never encapsulates untried possibility.

The artist typically takes up a stand, marking himself out by his consistent opposition to a different point of view. Instead he might try to contain all points of view within his own, even when he is only concerned to express a segment of what he understands as whole truth. The part will gain from the instinctual truth of the whole. Music works on emotion like magic but it can hardly express this perspective by itself. Conscious of itself magic can inspire new art forms.

Voodoo is a more magical art form than jazz, or even Wagnerian opera. Magic may be seen as a solution that does not involve subjection or conformity to someone else's vision.

Drawn to the ideal of the renaissance mage one may look down on popular versions of the occult. Yet the magician may wish to manipulate popular superstitions rather than merely despising them. Magicians like Eliphas Lévi and Macgregor Mathers showed much creative originality.

Integration of philosophy and magic.

Magic may be justified as superior psychotherapy, or as organising political concepts. Rationalistic magic can be compatible with scepticism and analytical philosophy. **Otto Neurath**, the logical positivist, hailed the end of metaphysics and predicted a return of magic. Jung was essentially against individualistic magic for the reasons the church is.

Magic

Carl Jung

JH

The sorcery discovered and described by anthropologists has its system and logic. Primitive magic is not essentially different from the more sophisticated and philosophical variants. There is the same service of the egoistic will. More than mere technology, it is like a spiritual defiance. The need for religion contrasts with the need for magic. Religious orthodoxy is felt as constraint on the will.

Because the magical approach of neoplatonism is designed to answer to human desires it does not exclude rationalism, even of the austerest kind.

We may read the story of how neoplatonic philosophy became Christian philosophy from the magician's point of view. If dogmatic belief opens up new experiences, then we try dogmatic belief. There is a point of view from which the distinction between faith and doubt vanishes. When faith is seen as satisfying desires it is a form of triumph.

Magic inspires cultural reform. It may legitimatise values as when the neoplatonic philosophy at the Renaissance opened up of new possible values and ways of living.

Magic as spiritual discipline.

Magic taps into the field of transcendental desires. The magician aspires to modes of perfection, degrees of clarity and confidence that are normally considered impossible.

The Renaissance was a time when magical wisdom was revered, and latent energies could find expression. *'As above so below'*. Correspondences operate throughout all fields of human experience. Art was to serve on many levels, the development of the instincts. Proud and confident like a mage, the artist could aspire to an all round grasp of a total world of experience. With this is to come an understanding of the creative energies, an esoteric wisdom discovering hidden connections and significances.

The magical doctrine of will is for practical use. Those who concern themselves solely with the understanding can speak of magic as a 'forbidden science'. A doctrine of will is not an aid to the understanding, nor is it

Magic

intended as such. A magical cosmology is not so much a metaphysic as means of acquiring power. Yet magic does not so much reject orthodox religion as use it as a point of reference and stability. It uses concepts which are arbitrary, long passages of gibberish (anathema to the understanding) barbarous names of evocation. Yet magic is not at all antithetical to understanding. Unlike the witch the mage does not sell his soul to attain power. Magical books are to be kept hidden from the unworthy.

We may want to say that the words used by others are empty abstractions whereas ours refer directly to realities. Can this be a real distinction? Naïve optimism contrasts with affirmationism. The advance in rational control means returning perhaps to something once known and since lost, like the rediscovery of Egyptian magic. Seeing magic as desire, it has the same revitalising force as religion.

The magician may aspire to all experience, or at least a representative sample of the most basic forms of it, to make them all accessible, brought under the power of his individual will, learning how to utilise the whole range of possible human reactions. The Renaissance culture of magic contrasts with our modern obsession with specialisation and separate, fragmented wisdoms. Then the whole wisdom would be brought into the pursuit of a specialised task. The eternal is brought down into the particular.

The magical art is guarded with supernatural terrors to protect against misunderstanding and vulgarisation. Magic- the realisation of all romantic hopes and ambitions, without losing hold of common sense. The magician must face down supernatural terrors and seemingly insuperable difficulties.

Magic includes the secret of playing on the suggestibility of a subject, working him up to an emotional pitch. Attractive ideas that appeal to you, are likely to have no appeal to others. Any number of exciting ideas you write down leave others cold. Magic can work through power of sympathy.

Magic and history

Much as we may appreciate the Blavatskyan or Rosicrucian myth of hidden masters or adepts, history is probably not really like that at all. But from a magical point of view all sorts of historical generalisations may serve according to circumstances. Taking the vast storehouse of possible human experience contained in history, magic is a means of tapping this treasure. It is a function of rational magic to offer emotional satisfactions for all points of view. There is a magical technique for safely visiting Hell, like Aeneas, Dante, Virgil, Odysseus or Bulwer's King Arthur.

Against St Augustine's purely negative view of evil there is the sort of magical dualism to be found in dissidents like William Blake. The evocation of evil spirits in **Goetic** magic is an attempt to affirm a world view which includes this possibility of negative experience, affirming malevolence, even the bad trip, without being destroyed by it. One seeks something higher than the Augustinian Heaven. There are magical techniques for satisfying pride.

With philosophy we gain control of magical forces rather than remaining subject to them. The way to overcome repressive values is though the magical philosophy, not through magical hopes, like utopian schemes. With a magical view of the world one need not disbelieve in immortality nor any other idea that may appeal to the minds of men. The magical freedom of all possible ideas holds out a hope of existence as pure joy.

Magic

A magical perspective brings the sense that the ideas current in society are manipulable. To a great extent our desires for culture and society may be met by a suitable modification of intellectual ideas. The beliefs and values we entertain may more than is usually realised be open to alteration in the service of the will. We may look at ideas insofar as their deployment answers to various public and private motives.

Throughout history the magician has been a recognised type. Many of his accomplishments were perfectly real, however dependent on the conventions of his society. Magicians appear in the foundation myths of Christianity. The gospel story of the journey of the magi is said to be derived from the visit of the magician Tiridates to Nero, who wanted to learn magic.

The magician may treat established religion as a medium for exploring everything, the emphasis being on the exploration not the central dogmas. While he may accept St Paul's epistles on the level of scientific documents; his real motive is the urge to satisfy an infinite curiosity. Magic involves the use of verbal formulae for the satisfaction of desire. Fascinated with Cabbalistic conjurations, numerology, esoteric and mystic codes, Christian occultists play with the name of Jesus seeking assurance that magic proves Christianity. On similar principles the magician is interested in the power of the seducer, with charisma, sexual seduction and hypnosis. Such concerns moved Dee, Cagliostro, even Casanova. Aleister Crowley expressed this archetype in twentieth century society. There is a complex that tends to go together, though sometimes there are bits left out. Some magicians are notable for their chastity.

Magic and morality

Notwithstanding his egoism, we can see the point of the pure and simplistic morality of the magician. There are things he gives up for the sake of the Great Work; some might appear as moral renunciations. The (good) magician, for example, forswears injustice, untruthfulness etc etc. He is not possessed by the unworthy motives that govern lesser mortals.

There are good reasons why the magician is not subject to such vices. His will is typically just because injustice is a weakness, a shortcoming, and what has he to do with shortcomings? There is moral weakness in the sacrifice of a long term for a short term gain. It is the will divided against itself. Part of the essence of his vocation is that such short term gains simply do not appeal to him, they are not desired, they would not satisfy.

He renounces injustice because he no longer feels inclined to commit it. All his activity serves his leading will. Satisfaction outside that major current is not possible to him. The apparent exception to this rule is

Magic

when his will, that is his major current, is concerned with overthrow or amendment of current moral conceptions. Then it is that ordinary virtues may come to appear limiting, restricting and need to be transcended. Strictly speaking this is a different question. What is involved are matters of symbolism and terminology. While generally the magician will probably prefer to be described as just, in specialised cases he may perceive the description as a limitation. This is not to say his is unjust in the original sense. The issue is the description that we are to apply to him.

There is a mass of experience the magician would like to tap. Yet he may be told that his very egoism debars him from some of the most valuable experiences. Zanoni has to renounce human love. If he wants that he must give up his powers and die.

Different forms of life are in conflict and use morality against each other. With the desire for openness to experience come horrible, seemingly insoluble dilemmas.

Some moderns interpret the true aim of magic, as ultimately just to stimulate creativity. They might see the production of original thought as the highest aim of man. Magic would have this purpose, seen against the framework of orthodoxy. The view of it as mere technology is balanced by a view of it as religion. For people who are in favour of religion, it may serve their ideological agenda.

Personality

A magus could be expected to be in control of his life. A reputation as an occult personality could be presumably be damaged by unhappiness. Bulwer's marriage was a disaster.

Sir Edward had a fine intellectual forehead. The veins often became plain in it, which he said was usual in the foreheads of sensitive persons. He had a slender hand like an Eastern's. This I remarked when he was showing the lines of marriage on it. "Look," he said, "they are all broken." His life was not without much sadness, though outwardly successful. (Katherine Thurston, Irish novelist – The Mystics 1907)

Personality

Bulwer was not altogether blameless in the matter of his marriage. Sometimes his own behaviour with his wife Rosina displayed episodes of shocking petulance.

For him his image was important and bears strongly on his claim to esoteric wisdom. If he is to be personally admired for this we have to see him as getting over his bad marriage. He is the sort of writer for whom permanent unhappiness would have been an objection. So it is reassuring to learn that he found other women. They even bore him children. With typical Victorian hypocrisy he largely kept this secret.

Shades of George Borrow

As a young man he spent a week living with a gipsy girl among the Romanies. He put Gypsies into some of his fiction.

Before the twentieth century Gypsies often conjured up images of enviable freedom as well as secret knowledge.

> *And barren demure Micah thinks (for I know her heart saith the Lord) that I chose base things when I sate downe, and eat and drank around on the ground with Gypseys, and clip't, hug'd and kiss'd them, putting my hand in their bosomes, loving the she-Gipsies dearly.* **(Abiezer Coppe 1649)**

When he first met her this one told Bulwer his fortune and astonished him with her accuracy.

Having avoided traditional schooling he retained a number of eccentricities of dress and manners. Without a wife to tell him how to dress he retained the dandyism of his youth which in a more sober age brought derision and even accusations of effeminacy.

Rosina went so far as to accuse him of sodomy with his old friend and fellow dandy Disraeli. For outrageous attacks like that he briefly had her locked up in lunatic asylum.

Baudelaire had much to say about the dandy.

DANDYISM IS THE LAST SHIMMER OF THE HEROIC IN TIMES OF DECADENCE.

Personality

THESE BEINGS HAVE NO OTHER STATUS, BUT THAT OF CULTIVATING THE IDEA OF BEAUTY IN THEIR OWN PERSONS, OF SATISFYING THEIR PASSIONS, OF FEELING AND THINKING.... CONTRARY TO WHAT MANY THOUGHTLESS PEOPLE SEEM TO BELIEVE, DANDYISM IS NOT EVEN AN EXCESSIVE DELIGHT IN CLOTHES AND MATERIAL ELEGANCE. FOR THE PERFECT DANDY, THESE THINGS ARE NO MORE THAN THE SYMBOL OF THE ARISTOCRATIC SUPERIORITY OF HIS MIND.

Baudelaire was influenced indirectly by Bulwer via Poe. Nineteenth century French dandyism was an English export.

Bulwer's weakness at the death of his mother goes beyond typical Victorian morbidity. There is unmanliness in his relationship to his daughter at this time.

His insistence on the feminine values of affection and unselfishness tends to undermine the idea of him as a proto Nietzsche. Christian values are seen as suitable for girls. This presents a dilemma. One may want women to be unselfish, but then their values infect those of the male. Yet to bring girls up to be egoists is to make them strident and jealous of their rights. See *The Coming Race* for his thoughts on that subject. He writes to his daughter Emily of his firm belief in the power of will. He needed women as muses, and tragically the way this was pursued clashed with Emily's needs. It is notable how religion and unselfishness seemed to be thought appropriate for females, though not for males.

Such dilemmas were a theme of *The Coming Race*.

The writing of which he was most proud was his epic poem *King Arthur*. It cannot be considered a success, learned and clever as it is; the limited conventions of his era are too obtrusive for the greatness to which he aspires. Nevertheless Tennyson, hardly a friend of his, praised him here for raising the intellectual level of the reading public, so preparing an audience for his own *Idylls of the King*.

Annie Besant wrote of her friend Leadbeater that:

"In his parents' home when he was a child he saw the great Occultist, Bulwer Lytton, and he remembers seeing a letter, lying on a table, drop to the ground and flutter along it to his hand, untouched by aught visible."

The romantic writers from whom Bulwer distanced himself with his rejection of Byron had shown considerable interest in the occult.

Precursors

There were a number of popular occult novels in circulation.

Vathek by William Beckford

The Monk by Matthew Lewis

Melmoth the Wanderer by Charles Maturin

Frankenstein by Mary Shelley the poet's wife, referenced Agrippa, Albertus Magnus and Paracelsus. Bulwer was acquainted with her but there was a falling out.

Honore de Balzac *Le Peau de Chagrin, Seraphita* and *Louis Lambert*

Francis Barrett whose book *The Magus* was published in 1800, held a school for magic in Marylebone, Barrett presented not just tradition but some explanation of how to do it, not just a book of spells to copy. But it was boring.

Early in his career Bulwer expressed a wish to read Albertus Magnus and Agrippa. Presumably he did, for he recognised Barrett's book as simply plagiarising large chunks from Agrippa.

An earlier work was Charles Johnson's *Chrysal of the Adventures of a Guinea* which had a Rosicrucian theme, as did Pope's mock epic *Rape of the Lock*.

Bulwer was proud of his ancestor, Dr John Bulwer author of *The Artificial Changeling* 1650 and *Chirologia* 1644.

Chirologia 1644 (J10.4)

> *He is not a genius, but his novels are marked with great energy and with a courage of experiment which in each instance had its degree of success. The story of Zanoni was one of those world-fables which is so agreeable to the human imagination that it is found in some form in the language of every country, and is always reappearing in literature. Many of the details of this novel preserve a poetic truth. We read Zanoni with pleasure, because magic is natural. (Emerson)*

Zanoni

Zanoni: *If I told thee that I could initiate thee into the secrets of magic which the philosophy of the whole existing world treats as chimera, or imposture, if I promised to show thee how to command the beings of air and ocean [...] thou wouldst listen to me then.*

Glyndon is a young man who seeks initiation from Mejnour the old hierophant, teacher of Zanoni himself.

Mejnour passed his hand over the young man's heart,—it beat loud, regularly, and boldly. He looked at him with something almost like admiration in his passionless and frigid features, and muttered, half to himself, "Surely, in so much courage the true disciple is found at last." Then, speaking aloud, he added, "Be it so; man's first initiation is in TRANCE. In dreams commences all human knowledge; in dreams hovers over measureless space the first faint bridge between spirit and spirit,—this world and the worlds beyond! Look steadfastly on yonder star!"

Psychedelic.

Follow me, then, and submit to the initiatory labours." With that, Mejnour led him into the interior chamber, and proceeded to explain to him certain chemical operations which, though extremely simple in themselves, Glyndon soon perceived were capable of very extraordinary results.

"In the remoter times," said Mejnour, smiling, *"our brotherhood were often compelled to recur to delusions to protect realities; and, as dexterous mechanicians or expert chemists, they obtained the name of sorcerers. Observe how easy to construct is the Spectre Lion that attended the renowned Leonardo da Vinci!"*

And Glyndon beheld with delighted surprise the simple means by which the wildest cheats of the imagination can be formed. The magical landscapes in which Baptista Porta rejoiced; the apparent change of the seasons with which Albertus Magnus startled the Earl of Holland; nay, even those more dread delusions of the Ghost and Image with which the necromancers of Heraclea woke the conscience of the conqueror of Plataea (Pausanias,—see Plutarch.),—all these, as the showman enchants some trembling children on a

Zanoni

Christmas Eve with his lantern and phantasmagoria, Mejnour exhibited to his pupil.

...

"And now laugh forever at magic! when these, the very tricks, the very sports and frivolities of science, were the very acts which men viewed with abhorrence, and inquisitors and kings rewarded with the rack and the stake."

"But the alchemist's transmutation of metals—"
"Nature herself is a laboratory in which metals, and all elements, are forever at change. Easy to make gold,—easier, more commodious, and cheaper still, to make the pearl, the diamond, and the ruby. Oh, yes; wise men found sorcery in this too; but they found no sorcery in the discovery that by the simplest combination of things of every-day use they could raise a devil that would sweep away thousands of their kind by the breath of consuming fire. Discover what will destroy life, and you are a great man!— what will prolong it, and you are an imposter! Discover some invention in machinery that will make the rich more rich and the poor more poor, and they will build you a statue! Discover some mystery in art that will equalise physical disparities, and they will pull down their own houses to stone you! Ha, ha, my pupil! such is the world Zanoni still cares for!—you and I will leave this world to itself. And now that you have seen some few of the effects of science, begin to learn its grammar."

Mejnour then set before his pupil certain tasks, in which the rest of the night wore itself away.

His attempt to re-enter these realms on his own is the old story of the sorcerer's apprentice. He falls into the clutches of a monstrous being.

"Thou hast entered the immeasurable region. I am the Dweller of the Threshold. What wouldst thou with

me? Silent? Dost thou fear me? Am I not thy beloved? Is it not for me that thou hast rendered up the delights of thy race? Wouldst thou be wise? Mine is the wisdom of the countless ages. Kiss me, my mortal lover." And the Horror crawled near and nearer to him; it crept to his side, its breath breathed upon his cheek! With a sharp cry he fell to the earth insensible, and knew no more till, far in the noon of the next day, he opened his eyes and found himself in his bed,—the glorious sun streaming through his lattice, and the bandit Paolo by his side, engaged in polishing his carbine, and whistling a Calabrian love-air.

Harriet Martineau wrote a key to Zanoni which impressed Bulwer enough to include it as an appendix in later editions. Martineau was a novelist, essayist and pioneer sociologist, rather fond of laudanum, like several of her contemporaries.

DWELLER OF THE THRESHOLD:—FEAR (or HORROR), from whose ghastliness men are protected by the opacity of the region of Prescription and Custom. The moment this protection is relinquished, and the human spirit pierces the cloud, and enters alone on the unexplored regions of Nature, this Natural Horror haunts it, and is to be successfully encountered only by defiance,—by aspiration towards, and reliance on, the Former and Director of Nature, whose Messenger and Instrument of reassurance is Faith.

Much as she saw herself as secularist, hers is one very Christian interpretation. Bulwer did not deny or endorse it, just let it stand.

Psychedelic delights

For the psychedelic voyager astral light begins to play, with peacocks turning to rose windows. He follows the light for a long time. Mosaic floors, abstract patterns, turn into indescribable architectural fantasies. Then Muslim fan vaults. He has the thought that there is something lacking in the abstraction of Islamic architecture, that it lacks focus. Mediaeval Europe, he feels, understood this light and how to coagulate it. He takes a childlike delight in beautiful craftsmanship...

Glyndon obeyed, and Mejnour retired into the chamber, from which there then slowly emerged a vapour, somewhat paler and of fainter odour than that which had nearly produced so fatal an effect on his frame. This, on the contrary, as it coiled around him, and then melted in thin spires into the air, breathed a refreshing and healthful fragrance. He still kept his eyes on the star, and the star seemed gradually to fix and command his gaze. A sort of languor next seized his frame, but without, as he thought, communicating itself to the mind; and as this crept over him, he felt his temples sprinkled with some volatile and fiery essence. At the same moment a slight tremor shook his limbs and thrilled through his veins. The languor increased, still he kept his gaze upon the star, and now its luminous circumference seemed to expand and dilate. It became gradually softer and clearer in its light; spreading wider and broader, it diffused all space,—all space seemed swallowed up in it. And at last, in the midst of a silver shining atmosphere, he felt as if something burst within his brain,—as if a strong chain were broken; and at that moment a sense of heavenly liberty, of unutterable delight, of freedom from the body, of birdlike lightness, seemed to float him into the space itself...

Suddenly at that thought,—through this space, in which nothing save one mellow translucent light had been discernible,—a swift succession of shadowy landscapes seemed to roll: trees, mountains, cities, seas, glided along like the changes of a phantasmagoria; and at last, settled and stationary, he saw a cave by the gradual marge of an ocean shore,—myrtles and orange-trees clothing the gentle banks. On a height, at a distance, gleamed the white but shattered relics of some ruined heathen edifice; and the moon, in calm splendour, shining over all, literally bathed with its light two forms without the cave, at whose feet the blue waters crept, and he thought that he even heard them murmur.

Psychedelic delights

Such a vision can be counted as one of the best things in life. It is what the saints called religious experience, to be obtained after long meditation. Someone who despises and dismisses mystical experience appears somehow inadequate, radically unenlightened, with so much to learn. They said acid was not for the "doers"; but who were the "doers" but shallow idiots? Much inspiration derives from the religious experiences of psychedelic trips. People criticised acid heads for despising consumer society while being dependent on its benefits. But why should the only revolution be an economic one?

BETTER CHANGE YOUR MIND INSTEAD...

...sang the Beatles.

In the hypersuggestibility of the threshold phase, the spirit is less free and has to submit to the yoke, tame its pride and arrogance. Passed through, one may be proud, antinomian. You rediscover your own ideas. Thinking may be quite intense. One takes pride in the idea of oneself as skilful psychedelic voyager. Having passed through the threshold, guided by such thoughts, one may find oneself on what is called "*the plateau*". After a while danger recedes, or appears to do so.

Having love, first fresh love of youth, hardly even conscious of it one takes it so much for granted that one can go on an ecstatic romp through the cosmos. There is pure triumphalism with no motive but delight, follow it and see where it leads, to what supreme triumphs. That was good, that was as good as anything in the history of the world.

Psychedelics are like magic; there is joy in thinking of oneself as an experienced magician. Mystical insight has subjectively the quality of a very clear, even intellectual idea, formed of the hallucinatory material in all its beauty and colour. Memory is important. One hopes the mystical state can be remembered properly. Its moral meaning is elusive. The psychedelic trance may appear to justify all. LSD was used by Argentinean torturers for the fascist regime.

> *"You may remember,"* said Julius Faber, *"Sir Humphry Davy's eloquent description of the effect produced on him by the inhalation of nitrous oxide. He states that he began to lose the perception of external things; trains of vivid visible images rapidly passed through his mind, and were connected with words in such a manner as to produce perceptions perfectly novel.*

> *'I existed,'* he said, *'in a world of newly-connected and newly-modified ideas.'* When he recovered, he exclaimed: *'Nothing exists but thoughts; the universe is composed of impressions, ideas, pleasures, and pains!'* (Strange Story)

Psychedelic delights

Timothy Leary wrote of a state of ultimate enlightenment:-

When the yogi attains final discrimination, renounces even that, he attains the condition called "Rain Cloud of Divinity". Mind without impurity and impediment attains infinite knowledge, what is worth knowing in this world becomes negligible...

...The dissolution of Qualities in their source, when nothing remains to be achieved, is liberation; the revelation of the power of Self, the foundation of the beauty of Self. (Patanjali aphorism book iv).

Psychedelic hierarchism involves an attitude of reverence towards an esoteric wisdom. The alternative is the psychedelic anarchism that breaks down all distinctions and refuses to go along with any hierarchies.

Taking the former path, one learns from the drug the significance of the middle ages. The spiritual world it set up with its devils and saints were in one sense representations of the bad and the good sides of possible hallucinatory experience.

The discipline imposed by the Catholic religion is something we can dispense with in coming to appreciate it and respond to it. We have to maintain balance by also responding to other religions, not as Jung put it, alien oriental palaces to which we have no right of access. That statement of his is mere dogmatic prejudice.

NEXT WE HAVE THOSE WHOSE CONSCIOUSNESS HAS GONE BEYOND GAME, GONE BEYOND DIRECT SENSORY AWARENESS, GONE BEYOND CELLULAR FLOW AND CONTACTED THE MOLECULAR AND ELEMENTAL ENERGIES THAT CRACKLE AND VIBRATE WITHIN THE CELLULAR STRUCTURE.

THOSE WHO HAVE TAKEN LARGE DOSES OF LSD, MESCALINE, DMT, AND EXPERIENCED WHAT THE EASTERN PSYCHOLOGISTS CALL THE "WHITE LIGHT," THE "VOID," THE "INNER LIGHT."

Psychedelic delights

JH

"WE ARE SURELY THE RIGHTFUL HEIRS OF CHRISTIAN (HEBREW, GREEK, AND GNOSTIC) SYMBOLISM, BUT SOMEHOW WE HAVE SQUANDERED THIS HERITAGE. WE HAVE LET THE HOUSE OUR FATHERS BUILT FALL INTO DECAY, AND NOW WE TRY TO BREAK INTO ORIENTAL PALACES THAT OUR FATHERS NEVER KNEW." (THE ARCHETYPES OF THE UNCONSCIOUS)

The mediaeval nobility wanted to create something together, somewhat divergent from the doctrines of monks and priests. Their Christianity was essentially something to make them feel good and giving assurance of salvation, a system for the coagulation of the light, with the confidence that all will be well. They developed their own version of it with the legend of the Round Table and the Holy Grail.

The middle ages explored a rich world of possible hallucinatory experience but this does not mean we need fall victim to its ideology to appreciate its achievement. We can, if it has to be that way, be heretics. Let us be several different kinds of heretic. The era was rich in unorthodoxies which nevertheless did not deny its angelologies and so much other highly aesthetic paraphernalia.

Perhaps it was a serious error to desire mainly the ecstasy. Perhaps the ecstasy is really a mere accompaniment of what should be desired. The will must continue to advance. The nature of the significant changes it undergoes must to be driven by the release of an overwhelming tension.

The drug brings an extreme stimulation of the experience of the beautiful. Pushed to a sufficient intensity, the beautiful becomes the religious and the mystical. As a pilot through life, one is to consider not simply the drive to fulfilment, but spare time for the enjoyment of the beautiful, particularly that generated by your own efforts to achieve satisfaction.

Horrors

The **Dweller of the Threshold** is the quintessence of what the acid heads call the bad trip.

After the joy of Sergeant Peppers came the bad trips. John Lennon turned to an extreme and depressing form of psychoanalysis to extricate himself.

Mejnour, the master, would insist there is light at the end of the tunnel. The obvious suggestion is that the pain and horror is something one should be able to live through; but it seems like the kind of thing that is in its very essence too horrible for that, something totally threatening and utterly destructive in a worse than mortal manner. However .the horror is always formed of the subject matter and symbols of society and civilisation.

To become a god one must become something unique, give a name to a force which has never previously been named. The misunderstanding of this uniqueness is yet another ingredient of the bad trip. To strive for uniqueness in face of the absolute is seriously insane.

This is fear run riot. You have cancer, you are about to be hanged, you are surrounded by black marias and policemen, all representing the reality to which you are threatened with waking up. This reality presents itself as perfectly real, you know how easy it would be for you to wake up to it, and forget everything you previously knew about your recent situation. This reality contains within it everything that is most absolutely horrible, most unacceptable, and you have to fight it off with your mind. You could not even yield to it, invite the policemen to come and take you off and hang you; they would recede at your invitation. They are not merely the physically visible embodiments of the quintessence of horror; the horror is a logical principle, the execution threats, the black marias which rev up at each jeering onset are merely its officers. Their object is not to kill you, but to inspire you with an absolute terror and despair. With respect to the real world you have involved yourself in the worst possible situation. you could possibly have involved yourself in; the sense impressions you receive convey the worst and most horrifying of all possible meanings. And this worst of all possible meanings somehow includes worse things than mere fear, things which depress the mind long after the fear has subsided. Remorse, nausea depression misery despair feebleness stupidity etc etc.

Horrors

There are no simple solutions. Leary's approach is hieratic and unconvincing to the rational mind. It is unappealing because it involves submission to an arbitrary idea of reassurance.

If anything is good then something has to be bad. Yet surely the root of the problem is not really philosophical but simply one of feeling good in general?

The bad trip means being plunged into a world of real living danger, or rather what is sensed as such. Biologically, pain is useful to the organism. The pain of disease is the effort at cure.

One is wide open, yearning to be reunited with one's missing half, as in the Aristophanes myth in Plato's *Symposium*, a lover like Lancelot or Tristram. Something like betrayal in this state of total weakness unhinges the mind.

LANCELOT AT THE CHAPEL

The subject may be proud of his bad trips, never having heard of anything so unique in its solipsistic horror.

Michael Wharton described his experience of the horror:-

"There are certain associated temptations. One is to invite the horror, to endure it because of the possibility, even the conviction, that what lies on the other side of that evil might be a counterpoising and transcendent good. But I have never had the courage

Horrors

to let go. The other temptation is less easy to resist; it is a certain pride at having sensations, however unpleasant , which are the privilege of few, the elect marked off from those who smile and call life pleasure. the pride is, I am certain, very dangerous, it is playing not with fire, but with evil itself."

Placing hell on a cosmic map, there is an idea of frustration being eternal and intrinsic. Sometimes aversion must strike out futilely. Truth as perceived will not prevail. This is true pessimism. There were always those who were broken on the wheel. Power prevails, not truth. There are no guarantees.

Try to face it rationally. The suggestion is that for the individual there is not necessarily any solution at all. He may have to believe in the possibility of a solution, but why should we assume there is one? This is to say there is to be no escape from intolerable annihilating pain. He has to believe there is a solution, this is the law of life, but why in the nature of things does there have to be? Consider the status of truth in a state of decadence. Given you have some powerful inner feeling, conviction or realisation, it ought to be possible to express this, to communicate, to make oneself understood. That would at least be an approach to a solution; at least you could hand on the torch, but suppose you meet with complete incomprehension, as if you are a being from another planet? And why should we expect that it is not so? Stupidity, we would want to say, it is they who are stupid. Or is it? But I fail to see any way in which I could have fallen into error. There is mutual aversion. Perhaps we are just different beings, perhaps I am a Martian.

The idea that in a common culture we could intelligibly map out our differences may be quite wrong. You might be right to see what is clear to you. Yet you might be totally ineffective through bad luck or something to that effect. Or was it the nothing the world deems it?

And what way is there of telling except that of having power? For to accept one's own nothingness is not possible. All that feeling, all that vision and understanding is to be cut short, frustrated. This is a philosophy of the bad trip. The memory may serve the will, as may aesthetic enjoyment, it may inspire it. Contemplation and memory are almost the same thing. Suppose that the primary aim of the will is to provide material for contemplation and memory?

I would not say this is just the will turning against itself. There is a corner of hell the world permits to exist. For hell is a nothing trying to be a something. There is not room for everything trying to exist that wants to exist; but madness is permitted to exist in a certain place (but not here).

Walking home becomes a nightmare, an ultimate situation. The situation seems the same, eternally repeated. Walk on, march boldly forward, keep them at bay, that's recommended. It's only dope, not acid, you can always pull through.

Like one that on a lonesome road,
Doth walk in fear and dread,
And, having once turned round, walks on,
And turns no more his head;
Because he knows a frightful fiend
Doth close behind him tread.

The components of the diabolic jigsaw, wanting to piss, excruciating shame, the woman at home, the numbers on the street doors, turning the key in the lock, taking a drug that opens the gates of terror.
Normal reality as understood dissolves into the solipsistic construction.

Each element of experience has bearing on this test, fraught with most frightful danger. The malevolent meaning of everything. It's here again. the test is

Horrors

actually impossible, surely. Only by suppressing it does life continue. Even walking boldly can seem to be one of the compensations of the jigsaw.

The horrors; *"the universe is a loaded gun pointed straight at your head."*

Bulwer associated them with the Dweller of the Threshold invoked by the ignorant sorcerer's apprentice.

It is conceivably worse when they come out of the blue, unconnected with the ingestion of any drug.
The compartments of life would have broken down and everyday living would involve fear and apprehension.

"Nothing is true" is no good as an all sustainer.
"Nothing matters" is just as bad.
In the Acid Trippers Dilemma, what the acid tripper continually tries to remember is his idea, that everything throws itself back into the same confusion.

This is the idea that will nearly get him home but not quite. You see if he were to do so it would amount to a proof of his idea, certainty for it. That is not good enough.

The great white light could be said to be past doubt. One must not stake anything on the final illumination. An idea is an affirmation of individuality. Fools ask you to explain what it is that is revealed to you.

The doubt all dilemma. Struggling to doubt all. As soon as I realised I was not doubting that I doubted all the collapse began to set in. So I was doubting and confidence returns to be shattered again. This was my hang-up. Now I was the acid tripper trying to get home, to escape from the nightmare. I knew my own thought processes well enough to realise well enough what I had to do as a temporary measure, to enable me to make a few more steps.

Now it is coming back to me in all of its horror. I had shut it out of my mind. It frightens me even now. This leads on to a horror death fantasy, which I hardly dare to think of I am frightened I might go off again. The thing is a screaming horror. It is not just policemen and straitjackets, it is room 101, that that which absolutely cannot be countenanced, a dilemma state represented by cosmic policemen, mocking voices.

Everyone asks what secret is revealed to you.
What is this horror of horrors, that sends terrible shivers throughout the body, the unthinkable, that which destroys mind and soul. I would like to say that what I went through was not merely a horrible trip, but the nightmare of nightmares. One can prepare for death, but how can one prepare for dilemma? How can I say I will abandon myself to the dilemma when the nature of it merely throws you from one horn to the other? I say this dilemma is ridiculous nonsense, there are no truths revealed under acid, dilemmas are a

Horrors

ridiculous idea. March on. So your chance of getting home depends on the success of this logic. Can I really believe this idea of mine If it is true it is true. If I do not believe in it is it is false. The world ends not in death but in dilemma. And how would I ever adjust myself to dilemma? What could happen but a breakdown of the mechanism. My dilemma is a logical dilemma. I am in a plane which is halted on logical dilemma. To people on a normal plane I am an acid tripper blowing his nut. But I know the universe has come to a nasty end in logical contradiction.
Everyone asks what secret is revealed to you. *What is yours?*
There is no secret.
Is that yours?
No!
What do you mean then?
Everything throws itself back onto the same confusion. Work it out if you can for yourselves, I don't know.
Ah! Your secret is agnosticism.
No!

It does seem to be rational thinking that is the hang up. I committed some of the sins of gross rationalism I should have known about.

One trips out on something, one must not be thinking about secrets and insights all the time. I imagine one can trip out on pure thought but certainly not in it, certainly one must not use it.

Nothing can be too bad, one says, but if logic breaks down this is an irrelevancy. The desire to be strictly logical detaches one's mind from anything in particular. One has to negate. The screaming horrified acid head is right. The end has come. The mind can no longer take it. This is the world prepared for you, part of the diabolical plot. Things are according to the experiences you have of them. Try to get away from it by denying it.

Try and abandon yourself to the forces of the dilemma, say "*ok madness is here*", you immediately begin to recover.

So this is your secret, how to get out of it? No, there is no secret. Someone under the drug is governed by the same laws as someone not on it. So this is the truth about it? It seems as if, in my effort to regain reality, escape the dilemma, I was only perpetuating it. Perhaps this was because I had certain tasks to perform like getting back home. I felt that if I gave myself up to free flow acid trip my behaviour would be so insane that I would be carted away. I wanted to enter the Houses of Parliament by the mps' entrance. So another part of the acid trippers dilemma was the acid tripper trying to get home. To get home it was necessary to think rationally. If the acid tripper gave way to his trip he would be seized by police. His mental agony would be eased but he would look a fool.

From *The Tibetan Book of the Dead* comes the observation that the essential goodness or badness of a trip is determined by one's karma before taking the trip and that efforts during the trip to make it good are irrelevant to whether it will be so. But it may appear as if such efforts have a bearing. Here we are faced with something very like the Christian problem of reconciling freewill and predestination and contemplation of it may help to understand something like mystical answers to the religious dispute.

Horrors

fear ceases. I may want to trust in nothing but my self created mythology and not to be bound absolutely even by that.

Allen Ginsberg, Leary and others offer their own explanations of the causes of a bad trip and what amounts to instructions for their avoidance. Objections to such schemes spring partly from the consideration that they seem to require faith, equivalent to a dogmatic theology in which one is expected to trust. It might be said they are just offering help.

There is danger in that they proffer a metaphysics and a cosmology within the framework of which we are expected to find relief and shelter. Trust in God and all

Anticipation

Alfred Richard Orage (1873 – 1934) ran the influential journal of British Modernism *The New Age* from 1907 - 1924. He was one of the main interpreters of Nietzsche for the British.

In those days it was possible for a well-meaning Englishman to be both a Nietzschean and a socialist. There seems to have been a genuine concern to relieve what was felt to be the distress of the common people, combined with a half plausible belief that a revolution could put it right. In addition Orage was a Theosophist, though he eventually fell out with the society. For him, Nietzsche was unquestionably a mystic, a member of the long and ancient tradition. Looking for Nietzsche's British precursors he found them in Bulwer-Lytton and Disraeli.

Writing in the *Theosophical Review* he is not especially impressed by Bulwer's mystical understanding especially when measured by the standard set by the Bhagavad Gita.

According to **T.S. Eliot,** *the best literary critic of his time.*

Nevertheless he thinks he is in some unconscious way wiser than he realises. Orage sees Mejnour as

Anticipation

anticipating Nietzsche's ideas about the Ubermensch despite Bulwer's rather different explicit intention of presenting an embodiment of ice cold intellect.

Is that vision of the future that awaits us, that splendid idealism, quite consistent with Lytton's Mejnour ? Such an ideal can be paralleled perhaps in the works of a real man, singularly like Mejnour in his apparent chilly isolation, and singularly like him too in his passionate devotion to humanity — Frederic Nietzsche ; and the parallel is almost complete when one finds Mejnour saying of himself, "my art is to make man above man-kind." Lytton's conception of Mejnour was as wrong as a man's comprehension of his own work can be ; and those who seek in Zanoni the lofty allegory of the two paths of Intellect and Devotion with the hope of finding them distinctly marked, will find more evidence in Lytton's intention than in his book. For those who realise the essence of Romanticism and the character of its literature there remains, however, a considerable value — though on lower slopes — in the meaning already suggested. For them Mejnour will represent not an individual at all, but a mood of Lytton's mind, standing out for awhile on the background of an emotional temperament ; a mood only dimly realised by Lytton himself, and utterly distasteful to his nature. Zanoni, too, is no individual but the symbol of the Mejnour-mood returning and becoming re-absorbed in the general colour of Lytton's mind — the intermediate type between Intellect as Lytton conceived it and Emotion as he felt it. The problem Lytton thus set himself to solve was in reality not the antagonism between Pure Intellect and Pure Emotion, but the reconciliation of two factors in his own personality which seemed to him mutually exclusive and destructive.

Orage was attracted to Nietzsche's ideas of will to power and the Ubermensch as well as life affirmation, and the positive valuation of desire. Although will was an important idea in much nineteenth century literature, setting a positive value on it came after a period of fashionable negation, the Buddhistic and Schopenhauerian view that art and enlightenment meant escape from the will. The sickness and death art of the decadents and symbolists needed Nietzsche for the switch to conscious affirmation.

Symbolism

Art in itself, if not necessarily typical, is essentially a suggester of something subtler than that which it embodies to the sense. (Zanoni)

Too plainly expressed, some very personal sources of pleasure risk sliding into the ludicrous or the disgusting. Hence all the poeticised sexuality of chivalry, grail legend, round table, rosy cross, etc. The object is not to reduce everything to sex; nor is the symbolism anything to do with guilt or repression. Read right this mediaeval symbolism is a form of lyricism. It is not so much that the meaning of the Arthurian legends is sexual, for the sexual itself is a symbol or figure of human happiness in all its manifold variety. Arthurian legend is closely involved with esoteric Christianity. Energies find expression within a more or less Christian framework of symbols and concepts.

The Pre-Raphaelites did not really promote the middle ages, only their own dream of it, which was in many ways tied to convention. Naturally they could not escape Bulwer's influence. One of the first paintings exhibited by the Pre-Raphaelite Brotherhood was *Rienzi Vowing to Obtain Justice for the Death of his Young Brother Slain in a Skirmish between the Colonna and Orsini Factions* by Holman Hunt, a scene from Bulwer's novel. 1849

For many years the group of artists around D G Rossetti were opening up new frontiers, creating a dream world that was a reflection of their responses to some of the art of the past. This was offered as escape, but it was still tied up in conventional judgements. They failed to detach their art from the values of mass civilisation as much as they intended. This had the consequence of contributing to the sickly piety of the Sunday school.

In the early eighties a movement of poets, artists, and café loungers in Paris came to form the Symbolist movement in art and literature. The highly charged imagery of occultism fed into this, helping to make sense of the disorder. Historian of the movement, **Arthur Symons**, suggested that the mad proto-Symbolist writer **Gerard de Nerval** who hanged himself in 1855, might have survived if he had really been versed in something like Kabbalah.

One seeks a philosophical underpinning for something that mostly did not articulate itself in such terms. To understand it one feels the need for a critic like Symons, but even more for Schopenhauer. In Symbolism we have art that offers consolation for a certain frustration of the will. It is an escape from unhappiness into something so different that it can seem like renunciation.

Symbolism

Another Symbolist painter, **Odillon Redon**, illustrated *The Haunted and the Haunters*.

Critics say of painter **Gustave Moreau** that he uses Symbolism for essentially private purposes of his own. Some have seen this as an anticipation of Freud. But the Symbolist is not necessarily content to see his vision as private. It affects religion and politics. It leads into hermetic philosophy and occult movements. The aesthetics of the later nineteenth century raises philosophical questions.

His black and white disembodied heads suggest mental disturbance. There is not an obviously formal beauty to his art, but then it is not that sort of painting. At first there seems no obvious message. One is in a dark world of madness and confusion. In his later work this changes and there is a definite movement towards

Symbolism

clarity and enlightenment. Seen in context the final flower paintings are beautiful, and symbolic of a kind of resolution. We recognise the function of much of the Catholic religious symbolism. He portrays women, boats, windows. Yet this does not lead into orthodoxy, it is freer and more eclectic. There are ventures into Hindu and ancient Babylonian mythology.

Symbolist paintings stand for a whole frame of mind. They are not intended to satisfy entirely in themselves. Unlike more conventional art, they lead beyond themselves to a world of thought and feeling. It is not hard to relate to; it is less like dream than reverie, subject to a degree of control. Certain kinds of images tend to resolve the chaos, to restore a happy serene state of mind; this the purpose of Symbolism. Obviously there can be a relation to Catholic orthodoxy which tries to take over but it can easily slip beyond Catholic control.

In England, Burne Jones was to illustrate the poetry of Robert, Bulwer's son. His religious painting can seem curiously blasphemous, the angels appear to wear lipstick, but this may be the effect of consumption. Burne Jones was an influence on continental Symbolists. We see how some of the problems he left unresolved became resolved in a different way.

Symbolist art invoked a form of magic as alternatives to many of the ideals of the French Revolution. Often the desired effect can be got only by a specific reversal of what is normally admired. The poet **Mallarmé** was into magic, as was his pupil **Rimbaud**. What had to be resisted was submission to the publicly received idea of happiness, by which one may be judged inadequate, perhaps sick; pressured to admire some ideal, some programme for living pushed by inferiors. To live in society is to dissent from it. Art offers an escape through an alternative ideal. Symbolists became decadents.

Mallarmé is associated with a symbolist reading of Wagner where political concerns are not prominent. Dreamy music provokes play of symbols which well up from the unconscious. They were created somewhere else; it is our minds that appropriate them, but a new unity is created.

Symbolism

Some ten or twelve years ago, a man with whom I have since quarrelled for sound reasons, a very singular man who had given his life to studies other men despised, asked me and an acquaintance, who is now dead, to witness a magical work. He lived a little way from London, and on the way my acquaintance told me that he did not believe in magic, but that a novel of Bulwer Lytton's had taken such a hold upon his imagination that he was going to give much of his time and all his thought to magic...

Sometimes an original force may be a disturbing and irritating one. Such was D G Rossetti's personality. Among his followers sentimental weakness let in much popular judgement, to overcome which became the task of a later generation.

The dream world has been offered as a solution. Comparing the Pre-Raphaelites with the men of the eighteen nineties, the Rhymers Club, Beardsley, Symons, Dowson and Yeats, the nineties had passed through the movement and discovered a kind of wisdom.

Symbolism

We should not think of the peculiar atmosphere of nineties London as only a lesser imitation of Paris. Here too there was a powerful and original creative mood, strongly opposed by conventional society.

A philosophy of renunciation left the Symbolist would-be mystic in danger of losing his way. Symons himself had a mental breakdown in 1908. Besides the risk of madness there was the problem of how to defend against the demoralising assaults of outside society. For some the solution was to be found in a vigorous egoistic aggression, drawing on resources like De Sade.

Immersed in such poetry as a believer, as one who feels the answers are there, to believe so strongly in art, in response to the sneers of the philistine one creates ever greater outrage. Protecting one's own vision, refusing to be beaten down. What is contemptible is only weakness.

The explicit ideals of poets were symbols of deeper realities. One's immediate social or political demands reflect one's immediate situation. They are the feelings to which one is provoked. To regard such objectives as the only important thing is to abandon art for politics.

Hidden in mystery is the power to bring a form of illumination. Perhaps this is part of the secret of Wagner, something that cold analysis simply misses. Sometimes when ideas can put us into a desirable state of mind there is a reason that is not entirely explicit in the ideas themselves. The ideas seem to be mere exoteric representations of an inner meaning which is the source of their power. Yet as soon as we try to analyse this to make it explicit, it evaporates.

Axel

Reading *Axel* by Villiers de Lisle Adam, this great classic of Decadent fin de siècle literature, if we are that way inclined we look for a philosophy behind it. We could see Decadent literature as an exemplification of Schopenhauer's philosophy.

Villiers began work on this dramatic poem in 1869 and was still working on it up to his death in 1889. He regarded it as his masterpiece.

For W B Yeats it was one of his "*sacred books*".

The plot has resemblances to that of *Zanoni*. Its alchemical and Rosicrucian themes are borrowed from that novel. If the *Tale of Two Cities* was one of *Zanoni's* progeny, *Axel* is another. In other works Villiers borrows much from Eliphas Lévi.

We can read *Axel* as a dramatic illustration of Schopenhauer's essential message of life negation and how it should be reversed. This pride, this rejection of everything ordinary, makes for an intensely aristocratic drama. What is rejected as "life" is really democratic vulgarity. Schopenhauer's own pride and pique finds dramatic expression. The mystical path is understood as a turning away from the common life. This is essentially a symbolic death; the refusal of life is a rejection of certain symbols. An intense pride takes to the limit its shocking rejection of normal values.

"Vivre? les serviteurs feront cela pour nous."
As for living, our servants can do that for us.

For the Symbolists art offered an escape into an alternative world. Whether as craft, as work, as dissidence, art contributes emotional and sensual support for a philosophy. We distinguish between art and propaganda. We can think of Schopenhauerian aesthetics less as pure essence of art, than as a religious programme that generates it, like Buddhism or

Axel

mediaeval Catholicism. This may be why Axel seems such a classic work. There is a theme of hubris. What God says to Satan is echoed by what the Archdeacon says to Sara. The poem well expresses the horror aroused by the Church, including the full arrogance of its claims. The old man of the forest raises echoes of Wagner's patron, 'mad' King Ludwig II of Bavaria, evoking feudal absolutism in a wonderful reactionary vision. Adding to this is the glory of ancient alchemical and hermetic lore, which is identified with life negation. It gives important sources of insight into Schopenhauer's pessimism, and into negation, and the Nietzschean point that this is really affirmation dishonestly described. We can see Schopenhauerian philosophy as offering a programme for an artistic culture, for the construction of works of art. The pure enjoyment, as described in Kantian aesthetic, ignores something that should not be ignored, the prior conditions that must be satisfied before aesthetic pleasure is possible. Finberg the translator says it is a tragedy. There is an obvious tendency to see it as preaching the unacceptable message of suicide.

Nietzsche himself manages the transvaluation by turning Schopenhauer into affirmation. He aspires to reproduce much of the effect of his philosophical predecessor while reversing his radical negation. Some however, still find Schopenhauerian rejection more aesthetic than the Nietzschean, prouder and more effective.

Some critics have wondered whether Bulwer might have read Schopenhauer. There is no evidence that he did. Although Schopenhauer had no direct influence on Bulwer, his philosophy dovetails neatly into some of his preoccupations.

As **Edmund Wilson** showed in his classic work of criticism, *Axel's Castle*, Axel and its themes were a key ingredient in the genesis of modernist literature.

The Magus

The magus is someone who lives in accordance with the precepts of esoteric wisdom, and is best placed to achieve his desires. Unlike the malevolent Mr Richards (*Haunted and the Haunters*) or Margrave (*Strange Story*), he is not just selfishly preoccupied with sensual pleasures; it is his will to do good and contribute to human progress. His influence may be predominantly scientific, like Paracelsus or Roger Bacon, or it may extend into politics like Merlin or John Dee. Political influence may be gloriously ambitious and doomed, like Giordano Bruno or Campanella's plans for the reform of Christendom, or even accidental yet effective, like Cagliostro's claim to have sparked the French Revolution with the Queen's necklace affair in 1785.

There is a potential clash between the wish of the magus to describe the nature of enlightenment and the desire to have followers who respect him for his wisdom. His achievement involves reputation in a way that seems to contradict strict Rosicrucian principles. He is much concerned with the cultivation of image. How to attract attention? How to acquire what people want? The claim to spiritual knowledge mixes with an element of charlatanry. Bulwer takes account of both aspects, expressing both scepticism and credulity.

Cagliostro
1743 – 1795

Real name Giuseppe Balsamo, Sicilian born occultist and adventurer who travelled all over Europe, including to London where he joined a Masonic lodge. He created a stir in various royal courts, and was allegedly mixed up in a plot to defraud Queen Marie Antoinette over a diamond necklace for which he was tried and acquitted. The extravagance and frivolity of the Queen revealed at the trial significantly lost her the sympathy of the French public.

Later in Rome, Cagliostro was arrested by the Inquisition and sentenced to death for Freemasonry. The sentence was commuted to life imprisonment and he died in prison.

> **"You have, you say, at your command the elixir of life of which Cagliostro did not leave his disciples the recipe..."** (A Strange Story)

The Magus

Here Bulwer follows Carlyle for whom Cagliostro was the Prince of Quacks.

To perfect himself in wisdom takes a long apprenticeship. Aiming at universal knowledge, the aspirant magus absorbs all contradictions into himself. He is above all straightforward definition. He wishes to understand and absorb the essences of all civilisations and cultures.

Plotinus is alleged to have gathered his wisdom in India. He reached total enlightenment, unity with the transcendent One, four times in his life. His pupil Porphyry only achieved it once, which should be enough for most people. For each the experience of mystical illumination can be whatever you take it to signify, but once achieved this supreme wisdom becomes something known, and others may aspire to it. When too many have succeeded there is need to posit yet higher understanding. Illumination must be something above and outside anything hitherto conceived. What the charismatic magus teaches must be something hard to imitate. The reputation he would like to establish for himself is not peaceful, not something he is happy to share. Yet even Plotinus would not want to be thought of as enlightened all the time. That would be too high; it would be indistinguishable from death.

Need I remind the reader that, while that was the day for polished scepticism and affected wisdom, it was the day also for the most egregious credulity and the most mystical superstitions,—the day in which magnetism and magic found converts amongst the disciples of Diderot; when prophecies were current in every mouth; when the salon of a philosophical deist was converted into an Heraclea, in which necromancy professed to conjure up the shadows of the dead; when the Crosier and the Book were ridiculed, and Mesmer and Cagliostro were believed. (Zanoni)

The Magus

Even while leading a disorderly life the magus may choose to present it as in all respects meaningful and noble, guides and signposts to help others through their own lives, symbols of illumination. You make your life into a myth, thinking how one may overcome appetite, to be driven not just by desires but by an aesthetic motive. There is something in common between the dandy and the magus.

This is another way in which the myth of the Renaissance Magus conflicts with strict Rosicrucian principles, some of whom like Paracelsus and Fludd, claimed to be virgins. Jennings hints that the chastity is not to be taken altogether literally:-

We have drawn to ourselves a certain frontier of reticence, up to which margin we may freely comment; and the limit is quite extended enough for the present popular purpose, — though we absolutely refuse to overpass it with too distinct explanation, or to enlarge further on the strange persuasions of the Rosicrucians.

A reason why esotericism has been so creatively fertile at times like the Renaissance is its popular mythic aspect, much of which runs as counter to materialistic science as much as any religious dogma. Yet the intellectual lumber may contain golden nuggets, and it helps to forge a relationship between magus and people. Men like Pico, Dee, Bruno, Fludd, Lull, Roger Bacon, were all lively clear-headed figures. An exception was Paracelsus who was nearly always drunk. In the popular mind is created the idea of some form of hierarchy of wisdom.

A magus may be very patriotic. What is the higher value, actually to have a history, a nationality, however good a one? Or to be in position to invent one? That is the real power of the magician.

Two Magicians

English alchemists, although fewer in number from those of some other countries, were of a notably high quality.

John Dee was the great magus, inspirer of the Elizabethan Renaissance and of English imperialism.

Angelic Conversations

John Dee and Edward Kelly's conversations with sprits took place as they travelled across Europe fleeing various dangers in the 1580s. Much of the original dialogue was recorded in Dee's diaries as published by Meric Casaubon in 1659.

With Kelly as his skryer, or crystal gazer, Dee had a number of fascinating conversations with spirits over a period of seven or so years , against a background of personal and political intrigue.

The subversive spirit Madimi first appears as a delightful charming child, so endearing to Dee that he names his own daughter after her. Later she grows into a sexually provocative subversive, appearing naked, teaching religious innovation and flagrant immorality, commanding Dee and Kelly to do a wife swap, which they do after overcoming much reluctance from Dee and the horrified reactions of the wives. Dee attempts to find theological and philosophical justification for the injunction.

Here is an extract from the diaries, Madimi manifests in Prague:-

☐. As I had talked of Madimi, and IL. to E.K. about Treasure hid in England: and I was desirous to have some advertisement by Madimi, she appeared.
Mad. ..... I answer your inward man. I am come again.
E.K. She is bigger than she was.
Mad. ..... I am a little grown.
☐. As concerning a medicine for my Ague, I would gladly ... And as concerning the wife of our dear friend, the Lor ...
Mad. ..... I pray you, bear with me at this time: I am as willing to answer you (when light cometh again) as you to ask me. You may consider of many things, I can answer them briefly. Such blessing as my Mother bestoweth on me, such I give you.
E.K. She smileth.
☐. God grant that his good Creatures may smile on me.
Mad. ..... When you know me well, you will find, I have been very charitable.
E.K. She goeth away naked; her body being besprent with blood; at the least that side of her toward E.K.

Was Dee just the dupe of Kelly, a very clever confidence trickster?

Bulwer's influence on the Victorian era is comparable to Dee's on the Elizabethans.

Alchemy

Michael Sendivogius - A New Light of Alchymy 1674

A New Light of Alchymy by Micheel Sandivogius 1674 (J9.10)

> *Sendivogius (1566–1636) was a Polish alchemist who discovered oxygen. At the court of Rudolph II in Prague, he got to know Dee and Kelly. Like several other alchemists he spent some time in prison.*

One of the worthiest modern efforts to uncover the meaning of alchemical symbolism was Jung's *Psychology and Alchemy*. One of his main sources was **George Ripley** (1415–1490). He wrote of him:-

RIPLEY BELONGED TO AN AGE WHEN GOD AND HIS MYSTERIES STILL DWELT IN NATURE, WHEN THE MYSTERY OF REDEMPTION WAS AT WORK ON EVERY LEVEL OF EXISTENCE, THEREFORE UNCONSCIOUS HAPPENINGS STILL LIVED IN UNTROUBLED PARADISIACAL PARTICIPATION WITH MATTER AND COULD BE EXPERIENCED THERE.

This was not the whole story.

George Ripley was an English alchemist who lived through the Wars of the Roses, the period covered in Bulwer's *Last of the Barons*.

Fifteenth century England has been described as a nation addicted to prophecy. In the previous century mystical speculation, individualistic and often heterodox flourished luxuriantly. Such mediaeval inwardness gave way in the fifteenth to an alchemical, style of thought fused with Arthurian fertility myth, focussing on the whole health of the community. Orthodoxy at this period was not what we understand from later, and there was not a protestant understanding of heresy and religious freedom. Heresy was considered a social nuisance, standing for religiosity and individualistic contemplative excess. In an unfortunate period of her history, England was identified with the Wasteland, with Henry VI as the impotent Fisher King. The character of his replacement, King Edward IV, including his virile sexuality, was deliberately created by government propaganda. In the twentieth century something of this fertility religion was revived by T S Eliot before his conversion to Christian orthodoxy.

Alchemy

One of Ripley's main sources were what have become known as pseudo-Lullian writings, (more pseudepigraphy). Much other alchemical literature survives, most of it obscure and the keys to decipher it have been lost.

There exist alchemical treatises that follow detailed instructions on the laborious procedures needed to produce gold and the elixir of life, with a casual remark that anyone who really takes any of it literally is wasting his time. The exact nature of the Great Work, the true aim of the alchemist was something shrouded in mystery. For the alchemist the mystic marriage of sulphur and mercury was the precursor to the achievement of the great work, symbolised as the manufacture of gold.

In such alchemical symbolism there is often psychological wisdom. The spirits sometimes summoned up in alchemical operations might include a choleric, hot tempered ruddy faced man. He represents hot-blooded youth and the necessity he perceives to satisfy his hot desires directly. With age he comes to understand alchemical possibilities of transmutation.

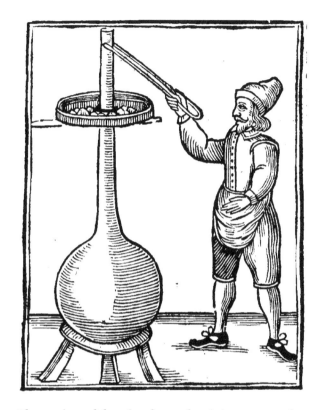

The ancient alchemists knew that it is not enough to perform an operation once for its full spiritual effects to be felt.

In the late nineteenth century August Strindberg practised alchemy in an unreconstructed form. His biographers tell us there were 50,000 practising alchemists in Paris in 1883. Later he came to feel that alchemy was a forbidden science, saying alchemists blasphemed God by trying to usurp his creative powers.

The Medium

Golden Dawn member and writer on mysticism **Evelyn Underhill** explained magic in terms of some axioms:-

The first axiom declares the existence of an imponderable "medium" or "universal agent," which is described as beyond the plane of our normal sensual perceptions yet interpenetrating and binding up the material world. This agent, which is not luminous and has nothing to do with the stars, is known to the occultists by the unfortunate name of "Astral Light": a term originally borrowed from the Martinists by Eliphas Lévi. To live in conscious communication with the "Astral Light" is to live upon the "Astral Plane," or in the Astral World: to have achieved, that is to say, a new level of consciousness. The education of the occultist is directed towards this end.

> **The Martinists were a school of Christian mystics founded in the eighteenth century by Martinez de Pasqually. Later it was refounded by Dr Gerard Encausse, aka Papus, another key figure in the French magical revival at the end of the nineteenth.**

To its devotees the occult is often a much wider and subtler subject than can be defined so dogmatically. For intellectuals outside the establishment elites like the Bloomsbury group, the occult itself was a *"medium"* for original and unconventional creative thought, in other words for dissident ideas to get a hearing. Nevertheless the concept of a physical medium was in some ways a fertile and productive one.

A great quack doctor comes out of Vienna and captivates the world with his theories. No, not Freud but Mesmer. Interestingly the mesmeric trance, or hypnotism, was not how mesmerism began. Rather it was a form of healing by *animal magnetism*. It took different directions, the occult and the scientific. Mesmer himself was dedicated to occult speculation in his later years.

Franz Mesmer

"THE GREAT THING OF THE EIGHTEENTH CENTURY IS NOT THE ENCYCLOPAEDIA, NOT THE SNEERING AND DERISIVE PHILOSOPHY OF VOLTAIRE, NOT THE NEGATIVE METAPHYSICS OF DIDEROT, AND D'ALEMBERT, NOT THE MALIGNANT PHILOSOPHY OF ROUSSEAU; IT IS THE SYMPATHETIC AND MIRACULOUS PHYSICS OF MESMER" (E LÉVI HISTORY OF MAGIC)

The Medium

The occult order integrates conveniently with the natural order. For Bulwer the analogy is electricity integrating with the laws of physics. He was impressed by how lightning, magnetism, static and fringe phenomena that one suspected might contradict Newton had been linked together by **Faraday's** discoveries..

It is so with the now familiar phenomena of mesmerism or electro-biology; the mind of the person operated on is affected through a material living agent. Nor, supposing it true that a mesmerised patient can respond to the will or passes of a mesmeriser a hundred miles distant, is the response less occasioned by a material being; it may be through a material fluid—call it Electric, call it Odic, call it what you will—which has the power of traversing space and passing obstacles, that the material effect is communicated from one to the other. (Haunted and the Haunters)

It aroused some interest in occult circles in nineteenth century Britain. In the absence of experimental evidence for its existence orthodox scientists came to reject it as pseudoscience, like phrenology, a study which also caught Bulwer's attention.

Oriental magic also includes the notion of a psychophysical medium, Lévi's astral light resembles the *Man Akasa* of the Hindus. It appears to be a magically useful postulate, and should not be immediately rejected as a piece of pseudoscience.

Odic Force: influenced by the works of Mesmer and Swedenborg, the eminent German scientist Dr. Carl Ludwig von Reichenbach (1788 – 1869) believed he had discovered an important new natural principle. Related to electricity, heat and magnetism, Odic force was a vital principle permeating and connecting all life, and detectable as an emanation from most substances. Sensitive subjects could see it as an aura, given sufficient practice. The concept was similar to oriental ideas like prana and was used to explain hypnotism.

The Medium

Francis Barrett insists on magnetism, a scientific medium to enable magical operations to be performed without the direct intervention of the Devil.

Mejnour professed to find a link between all intellectual beings in the existence of a certain all-pervading and invisible fluid resembling electricity, yet distinct from the known operations of that mysterious agency—a fluid that connected thought to thought with the rapidity and precision of the modern telegraph, and the influence of this fluid, according to Mejnour, extended to the remotest past,—that is to say, whenever and wheresoever man had thought. Thus, if the doctrine were true, all human knowledge

became attainable through a medium established between the brain of the individual inquirer and all the farthest and obscurest regions in the universe of ideas. Glyndon was surprised to find Mejnour attached to the abstruse mysteries which the Pythagoreans ascribed to the occult science of NUMBERS. In this last, new lights glimmered dimly on his eyes; and he began to perceive that even the power to predict, or rather to calculate, results, might by—(Here there is an erasure in the MS.)

In a letter to his friend Forster Bulwer declared mesmerism to be "*a mere branch current of the one great fluid pervading all nature*".

Strange Story

Doctor Allen Fenwick, the narrator, espouses the materialistic philosophy of Condillac, contemptuous of anything smacking of the occult. He is summoned to the deathbed of Dr Lloyd who accuses him of wrecking his life "...*in the bigotry which adds crime to presumption, you would stone the discoverer who, in annexing new realms to her chart, unsettles your arbitrary landmarks.*"

"SUDDENLY I FELT MY ARM GRASPED," ETC.

From the dervish Haroun of Aleppo, the great traveller Sir Phillip Derval has obtained some powders which appear to have miraculous properties. Under their influence Fenwick is shown in a vision his charming new acquaintance Margrave as he was before he took on his current body, as prematurely aged reprobate

Louis Grayle. Afterwards he asks to take away the powders for analysis but is refused. This annoys him.

As it is, I decline the confidence with which you would favour me, subject to the conditions which it seems you would impose. My profession abandons to quacks all drugs which may not be analyzed, all secrets which may not be fearlessly told. I cannot visit you at Derval Court. I cannot trust myself, voluntarily, again in the power of a man, who has arts of which I may not examine the nature, by which he can impose on my imagination and steal away my reason."

He does visit his house after Derval has been murdered:

We had now come to the end of the state apartments, the last of which was a library. "And," said the old woman, "I don't wonder the gentleman knew Sir Philip, for he seemed a scholar, and looked very hard over the books, especially those old ones by the fireplace, which Sir Philip, Heaven bless him, was always poring into.

Mechanically I turned to the shelves by the fireplace, and examined the volumes ranged in that department. I found they contained the works of those writers whom we may class together under the title of mystics — Iamblichus and Plotinus; Swedenborg and Behmen; Sandivogius, Van Helmont, Paracelsus, Cardan. Works, too, were there, by writers less renowned, on astrology, geomancy, chiromancy, etc. I began to understand among what class of authors Margrave had picked up the strange notions with which he was apt to interpolate the doctrines of practical philosophy.

112

Strange Story

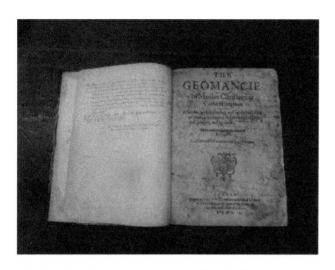

The Rosicrucians were concerned with living forever, but were *always prepared (nay, enjoined) to do good, wherever possible or safe.* (Jennings). *A Strange Story* is about this desire in the hands of someone evil, the sorcerer Margrave, who lives for sensual pleasure alone, having the mentality of what we might today call a psychopath.

Like Mr Richards in *The Haunted and the Haunters* Margrave has discovered a magical means of evading death indefinitely. The concept of the elixir of life is of the greatest interest to occultists.

But with respect to centenarians, some persons have been mentioned as having survived for hundreds of years, moving as occasion demanded from country to country; when the time arrived that, in the natural course of things, they should die, or be expected to die, merely changing their names, and reappearing in another place as new persons--they having long survived all who knew them, and thus being safe from the risk of discovery. The Rosicrucians always most jealously guarded these secrets, speaking in enigmas and parables for the most part; and they adopted as their motto the advice of one of their number, one of the Gnostics of the early Christian period: 'Learn to know all, but keep thyself unknown'. (Jennings)

Philalethes, Eugenius. F.R.S. (Actually Thomas Vaughan, hermeticist and brother of Henry the poet) Long Livers A Curious History of Such Persons of Both Sexes who have Lived Several Ages and Grown Young Again with the Rare Secret of Rejuvenescency of Arnoldus de Villa Nova. 1722

In an essay *St Germain the Deathless*, Andrew Lang, the Scottish poet and folklorist, famous for his collections of fairy tales, claims a source for the characters of Margrave in *A Strange Story* and Richards in *The Haunted and the Haunters*, rightly judging the latter figure the superior creation.

The Comte de St Germain was a mysterious adept who was alleged to have lived for centuries, possessing both the philosophers stone and the elixir of life. Lang goes so far as to suggest Bulwer might have known this adventurer who *"had drunk at Medmenham with Jack Wilkes"* in the middle of the previous century.

Strange Story

John Wilkes Esqr.
Drawn from the Life and Etch'd in Aquafortis by Wm. Hogarth.

Did Saint-Germain really die in a palace of Prince Charles of Hesse about 1780-85? Did he, on the other hand, escape from the French prison where Grosley thought he saw him, during the French Revolution? Was he known to Lord Lytton about 1860? Was he then Major Fraser? Is he the mysterious Muscovite adviser of the Dalai Lama? Who knows? He is a will-o'-the-wisp of the memoir-writers of the eighteenth century. Whenever you think you have a chance of finding him in good authentic State papers, he gives you the slip; and if his existence were not vouched for by Horace Walpole, I should incline to deem of him as Betsy Prig thought of Mrs. Harris. (Andrew Lang- St Germain the Deathless)

Medmenham in Buckinghamshire was the site of Sir Francis Dashwood's mock monastic order popularly known as the Hell fire Club.

Other works

In several of his historical novels magicians have a significant role in battles.

A Muslim sorcerer appears in his 1838 romance *Leila or the Siege of Granada*:-

Moorish towns, which had submitted to Ferdinand, broke from their allegiance, and sent their ardent youth and experienced veterans to the standard of the Keys and Crescent. To add to the sudden panic of the Spaniards, it went forth that a formidable magician, who seemed inspired rather with the fury of a demon than the valour of a man, had made an abrupt appearance in the ranks of the Moslems. Wherever the Moors shrank back from wall or tower, down which poured the boiling pitch, or rolled the deadly artillery of the besieged, this sorcerer--rushing into the midst of the flagging force, and waving, with wild gestures, a white banner, supposed by both Moor and Christian to be the work of magic and preternatural spells--dared every danger, and escaped every weapon: with voice, with prayer, with example, he fired the Moors to an enthusiasm that revived the first days of Mohammedan conquest; and tower after tower, along the mighty range of the mountain chain of fortresses, was polluted by the wave and glitter of the ever-victorious banner.

In *Harold* there is Hilda the noble Danish Vala, or female shaman.

The magic of Hilda was rather akin to the old Cimbrian Alirones, or sacred prophetesses; and, as with them, it demanded the priestess—that is, the person without human ties or emotions, a spirit clear as a mirror, upon which the great images of destiny might be cast untroubled.

However the natural gifts and native character of Hilda might be perverted by the visionary and delusive studies habitual to her, there was in her very infirmities a grandeur, not without its pathos. In this position which she had assumed between the earth and the heaven, she stood so solitary and in such chilling air,—all the doubts that beset her lonely and daring soul came in such gigantic forms of terror and menace!—On the verge of the mighty Heathenesse sinking fast into the night of ages, she towered amidst the shades, a shade herself; and round her gathered the last demons of the Dire Belief, defying the march of their luminous foe, and concentering round their mortal priestess, the wrecks of their horrent empire over a world redeemed.

In the *Last of the Barons* there is Friar Bungay, who raises a mist at the battle of Barnet to aid the Yorkists.

This Friar Bungay was a historical figure, a 15th century magician who must be distinguished from his better known namesake, who assisted Roger Bacon in constructing his brazen head.

More prominent in this book are the alchemist Warner and his daughter Sybil.

Other works

Alchemy was an important subject in the England of that time.

In the poem *King Arthur*, of course there is Merlin:-

The solemn Merlin — from the midnight won
The hosts that bowed to starry Solomon.

Of Solomon it is said:-

King Solomon bound the 72 evil spirits of the Goetia into a brass vessel solely because of their pride. Those of Babylon broke open the vessel and the spirits escaped.

For the esoterist this has a deep meaning. Solomon was a monotheist, ruler of a monotheistic empire, Babylon was curiosity and magic, open and polytheistic.

Solomon imprisoned the spirits to do honour to his own God, because the spirits claimed to be self subsistent, so presenting a challenge to his system.

His motive was not fear but aesthetic. Babylonian magicians replaced monotheistic restraint with a personal and individual protection. No longer are unorthodox experiences forbidden. You may have them so long as you guard yourself against possible evil effects.

Will

The will of man is the very being (esse) *of his life, and his understanding is the existence* (existere) *of his life therefrom.* (Swedenborg)

The idea of will pervades Bulwer's writing. He did not need Schopenhauer to teach him its importance. The importance of the will had long been a central tenet of occult philosophers.

The following quote will be familiar to readers of Poe, who was not only an enthusiastic admirer of Bulwer but sometimes counted as his disciple.

"And the will therein lieth, which dieth not. Who knoweth the mysteries of the will, with its vigor? For God is but a great will pervading all things by nature of its intentness, Man doth not yield himself to the angels, nor unto death utterly, save only through the weakness of his feeble will."

Joseph Glanvill was a seventeenth century occult writer who belonged to the circle of the Cambridge Platonists. Bulwer possessed his book on witches. Glanvill is ingenious in his defence of witch beliefs. He argues against a scepticism which would make *wise judges* into murderers.

Matthew Arnold's poem *The Scholar Gipsy* is a story taken from Glanvill.

For Evelyn Underhill's axioms of magic:-
(2) That there is an established analogy and equilibrium between the real and unseen world, and the illusory manifestations which we call the world of sense.

(3) That this analogy may be discerned, and this equilibrium controlled, by the disciplined will of man, which thus becomes master of itself and of fate.

In fact the whole culture of the occult is designed to serve the will. For intellectuals outside the establishment, people like the two friends Machen and Waite, it offered a medium for getting unorthodox ideas across. For Aleister Crowley Magick [sic] was *the science and art of causing changes to occur in accordance with the will.*

FOR PURE WILL UNASSUAGED OF PURPOSE, DELIVERED FROM THE LUST OF RESULT, IS IN EVERY WAY PERFECT.

The Coming Race

Margrave, Richards and Zanoni all exemplify willpower raised to the highest degree of magical intensity. The first two are evil but Zanoni is the good version. *The Coming Race* presents a synthesis of some of Bulwer's thoughts about will in the social form of a dystopia. Here is pessimism different from his generally positive view of the ideal world of the soul, which inspired Symbolists and Decadents. The story is set inside a hollow earth among a people called the Vril-ya, whose women are taller than the men and dominate with the use of a deadly form of energy called Vril. In these aesthetic and moral visions alchemical symbolism mixes with the horror of America.

This is his work of science fiction, one of the prototypes of the genre. The idea of the magical medium, the astral light, is turned into Vril, the energy source of the future. Vril is an expression of Bulwer's thoughts on the magical medium, and in a letter to his friend Forster he explains that he is thinking more of electricity than the animal magnetism of the mesmerists.

The Coming Race

The narrator is an American, a foil for the new order, expressing democratic values somewhat in advance of those in vogue in contemporary England. The Vril-ya take to an extreme new tendencies of the age, like the feminist ideas about reversal of gender roles that Ibsen was soon to make fashionable. Here too was the fatal woman who was to obsess the Symbolists and Decadents. Running out of space, it is expected the Vril-ya will soon emerge onto the surface of the earth and exterminate mankind as an inferior species.

Typically up to date with scientific thought, Bulwer melds fashionable racial anthropology with phrenology.

Their conformation of skull has marked differences from that of any known races in the upper world, though I cannot help thinking it a development, in the course of countless ages of the Brachycephalic type of the Age of Stone in Lyell's 'Elements of Geology,' C. X., p. 113, as compared with the Dolichocephalic type of the beginning of the Age of Iron, correspondent with that now so prevalent amongst us, and called the Celtic type. It has the same comparative massiveness of forehead, not receding like the Celtic—the same even roundness in the frontal organs; but it is far loftier in the apex, and far less pronounced in the hinder cranial hemisphere where phrenologists place the animal organs. To speak as a phrenologist, the cranium common to the Vril-ya has the organs of weight, number, tune, form, order, causality, very largely developed; that of construction much more pronounced than that of ideality. Those which are called the moral organs, such as conscientiousness and benevolence, are amazingly full; amativeness and combativeness are both small; adhesiveness large; the organ of destructiveness (i.e., of determined clearance of intervening obstacles) immense, but less than that of benevolence; and their philoprogenitiveness takes rather the character of compassion and tenderness to things that need aid or protection than of the animal love of offspring.

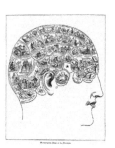

Esotericism

The Neapolitan philosopher **Giambattista Vico** attacked the idea that the mythology and symbolism of our forefathers contain an esoteric wisdom, as well as the popular idea that the men of the past were ruled by elites of sages. Their thought forms, he says, were simply more primitive than ours. We cannot really learn from them except about the genesis of ourselves. This viewpoint can be depressing and sterilising. Less so is his idea is that the object of historical investigation is to uncover what men thought, rather than simply classifying what happened according to our own schemes.

Vico echoes the Puritanism of emergent middle classes who want to differentiate themselves from the mass, as they do all over the world. He speaks up for moral restraint, for respectable virtues. He attacks the idea of esoteric wisdom of Homer, as well as the heroic morality in the aristocratic spirit of his own age. He has no time for Iamblichus.

Against this attitude is the hope there might be a vast amount one could learn from people of very different religious and cultural backgrounds. Esoteric wisdom is discerned in the obscurities of the Great Pyramid. I may feel I would like to read the runes or, like Blake, to share a drink with the man who built the pyramids. Perhaps we would have much in common.

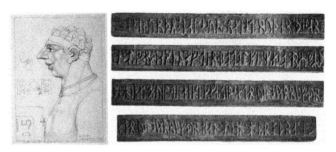

Esoteric philosophers may say things that on the face of it quite contradict each other, but they have an interest in feeling they can all communicate with each other and share something in common.

ALL RELIGIONS ARE ONE.

...says William Blake.

Sectarian enthusiasts disagree. Blake could have found mystics from other religions to concur with him on this, concerned as he is to minimise sectarian controversy. They look for agreement, unity, not points of dispute.

Esotericism

They come from diverse traditions but they agree. What do we make of it?

Bulwer was well aware of Blake. He was a friend of the artist **John Varley**, who had been a member of Blake's circle and told him all about the personality of the master. Varley was with Blake when he made his sketches of the man who built the pyramids and other spiritual beings.

Shakespeare still speaks to modern man because he was not altogether constrained by doctrine. His plays contain important elements of occult philosophy, but they are nothing like manifestos. He is more interested in the human soul than in advocating cultural reform. We revere him because of his psychological insight. Many have observed that Shakespeare does not come across particularly as a Christian. The occult philosophy itself is usually unfanatical and often compatible with paganism. For it evangelical Christianity becomes merely a piece of magic, or a supposedly scientific fact about the universe. Shakespeare's reputation for immense wisdom survives because he has no clear philosophy. It could not do so if we were really convinced he was Francis Bacon, Lord Verulam, with the definite views he identified with.

How can Christians look sympathetically at their descendants who will not be Christians? If meaningful understanding is to cross the barriers of different beliefs and values then some form of esoteric interpretation is called for. We often have to disregard the literal statement, which causes mutual incomprehension, and put an interpretation on it.

We may honour our ancestors, even worship them, but what would they think of us?

The origins of Christianity among the downtrodden classes of the Roman empire may lack appeal. Hymns may be found aesthetically repellent, Christian morality, especially on sexual matters, suffocating. But the religion can offer exalted spiritual feelings, and to an extent these may even come from or depend on an orthodoxy that repels.

Esotericism

Esoteric Christianity has much to be said in its favour. Where doctrine is essentially symbolic, the pain of decadence, looked at differently, is the birth agony of creation.

A society that actually takes seriously the formulae of modernity is one that has lost its esoteric side. The career woman has no time for the esoteric. She wants to be valued by the clear and explicit rules of an easily understood game.

Those who consider themselves successful want everyone to observe the rules of such a game. The British way has generally been to import modern ideas carefully, treat them with a healthy scepticism. This may be changing.

The esoteric is concerned with the procurement of hidden sources of satisfaction. The path is not of interest to the healthy minded who may themselves have mystical experiences that are fully satisfying, yet need only the simplest theory to explain them.

The esoteric has an intensely personal and individual character. The analogy with sexual seduction is close. Within the realm of the esoteric coercive generalisations no longer apply. That is to say there is no doctrine, no external truth to which you have to adapt. Once discovered, esoteric truth is deeply satisfying and enjoyable.

Esoteric wisdom is a type of total enjoyment, but it is one's own enjoyment, the result of surmounting personal obstacles. It may be conceived as the satisfaction of demands that not every personality type would feel impelled to make.

There are different interpretations of the Christos.

THE VISION OF CHRIST WHICH THOU DOST SEE IS MY VISION'S GREATEST ENEMY.

The democratic egalitarian Christ of the gregarious crowd opposes the Gnostic esoteric Christ of those who feel the primary thing is to escape the pressure of the gregarious crowd.

Esotericism

For the esotericist, art forms, buildings, historical events all present an esoteric significance. All are symbols. Everywhere hidden meaning is discoverable far below the surface. Esoteric Christianity is different, even opposite, to gospel Christianity. Gospel Christianity is moralistic, accusatory, ideological, shirty. Esoteric Christianity deals with historical forms and energies. The hidden emotional content of some form or appearance may be precisely opposite to what it is at first sight.

Thus the origins of Christianity, this fact of history which many find distasteful, and which orthodoxy cannot escape, is faced full squarely by esoteric Christianity as one of the mysteries.

That the occult and esoteric tradition in western civilisation has had a seminal and fertilising effect on mainstream exoteric developments suggests that thought does not have to proceed so much by trial and error as our conventional historians suppose. Perhaps there is a logic, or several logics governing creative originality. There are ways of thinking which are not intellectually respectable and which should certainly not become so, but which at certain points are capable of such clarification as to inspire discoveries of exceptional genius.

Some esoteric wisdom is to be found in almost every age. Its aim perhaps is to bring under the power of the will all the various possible basic forms of experience. This is to be achieved by a number of special disciplines which transcend the particular culture in which its aspirant finds himself a part.

The world's great sages are less conflicting than they are united. There is a common interest against confusion and stupidity which outweighs their respective differences. Clarity of expression itself brings unity, most radical disagreement comes from fuzzy thinking. When all positions are made clear, then real hatred is impossible.

All the sages could be reconciled. Ideas could remain as beautifully delineated possibilities belonging to the world of strife, while the real source of happiness lies in the freedom bestowed by a framework of symbols.

Esoteric philosophy is not like a scientific or philosophical theory, it is like a map. *"Theories are essentially argumentative systems of statements, their main point is that they explain deceptively. Maps are not argumentative"* (Karl Popper). Thus even the

argumentative nature of some esoteric philosophy is
not necessarily what it seems.

Esoteric philosophy is beyond all theory, its object is to
be a map, its argument may be a part of its
maplikeness, the only question to arise is whether it is a
good map or a bad one, not whether it is true or false.

Beyond a mere academic study, a history of prohibited
ideas can supply usable weapons. Esoteric learning is
commonly subversive, always for the few, and gives a
distinctive perspective. There are ideas that have gone
against orthodoxy throughout most of history, yet have
had profound underground influence. From the
premise that received opinion is limited or mistaken
derives a very powerful alternative tradition that is not
usually traced. Orthodoxy reacts strongly against a
philosophy radically critical of the civilisation it stands
for. Seen as insignificant or foolish, its possibility is
usually denied. Opposed to conventional wisdom,
esoteric wisdom appeals to a personality that has rarely
found favour. A heretical dissident mentality explores
censored ideas and revives the old wars between magic
and religion.

Yet the esoteric is not inevitably at odds with orthodox
religion. One example of an esoteric Christian is Karl
von Eckartshausen (1752 – 1803) author of *The Cloud
in the Sanctuary* which had some influence on the
Golden Dawn and made a contribution to the idea of

the Secret Chiefs, developing
and applying the idea of
initiation. His is a Christian,
even Catholic idea, but
exportable into other religious
positions. Eckartshausen (who
incidentally reveres Kant)
writes like a Rosicrucian
initiate or a member of the
Illuminati, Catholicised.

Victorian Gothic

At Knebworth Bulwer inherited a Tudor mansion and remodelled it into a gothic extravaganza.

Knebwworth East Front. 1878

Gothic Architecture. This term was originally applied to the mediaeval styles at the time of the Renaissance of the Pagan orders: some say it was first given by Sir Christopher Wren, but it is now believed to be older than his time. In any case it was given as a term of reproach and contempt at a time when it was also the fashion to write Latin, and to expect it to become the universal language. But the different nations of modern Europe have retained their respective languages in spite of the efforts of the pedants of the sixteenth century, and have now generally returned to their national styles of architecture also.

The one seems to follow naturally from the other: if the Roman language could neither be preserved everywhere, nor effectually revived, so also the permanent establishment of the Roman architecture was not to be expected. The marvel is that modern Europe submitted so long to its trammels. (John Henry Parker, 1846)

How can the Victorian be other than a romantic? This writer felt that the gothic revival was the restoration of a native style after the interruption of pseudo-Roman revivalism, but what concept of illumination did he have? Something more visionary was hinted by figures like Hargrave Jennings, William Blake, even Lewis Carroll, and eventually found explicit expression in surrealism.

Victorian Gothic

At an exhibition of Pugin's work we may feel we can understand why he went mad. Pugin's gothic "correctness" meant slavish imitation of the middle ages. His militant Catholicism can repel. If that is where his aesthetic vision leads then we draw back. Pugin's designs are pretty enough, but they do not express a mediaeval world view, only a romantic fantasy that takes itself a bit too earnestly.

Schopenhauer wrote of the gothic style:-
Whereas in ancient architecture the tendency and pressure from above downwards are represented and exhibited just as well as those from above downwards, in Gothic architecture the latter decidedly predominates. From this arises that often observed analogy with the crystal, whose formation also takes place with the overcoming of gravity. Now if we attributed this meaning and fundamental idea to Gothic architecture and thereby tried to set it up as the equally justified antithesis to classic architecture, it would have to be remembered that the conflict between rigidity and gravity, so openly and naively displayed by ancient architecture, is an actual and true one established in nature. On the other hand, the entire subjugation of gravity by rigidity remains a mere pretence, a fiction testified by illusion. Everyone will easily be able to see how the mysterious and hyperphysical character attributed to gothic architecture arises from the fundamental idea here expressed and from the above mentioned peculiarity of their architecture.

Hyperphysicality

In gothic cathedrals it is common to feel a sense of mystical illumination. To call it simply "emotion" seems to degrade it. One feels those Victorians did not understand what they thought they did, that their

Victorian Gothic

"mystical emotion" was mere romantic indulgence but that we have something like psychedelic understanding which is not an emotion.

"When he (St Bernard) said that the spectacle of the Cluniac churches reminded him of the old rites of the Jews, he was passing an adverse judgement on the whole Cluniac interpretation of the monastic vocation and of the Christian life, but he also implied a judgement on Cluniac art. The stiff and grandiose Romanesque manner, with its gorgeous, but palpably extraneous ornament, was simply no longer in touch with the spirit of the age." (George Henderson - *Gothic* p 72)

The young Burne Jones was fascinated by the gothic cathedrals of northern France.

This was an entirely admirable and worthy interest, and it is not for anyone to say that he or others like him misunderstood. They responded in a strong emotional way to one of the strongest strains in our heritage. It is not hard to tell ancient stained glass from nineteenth century imitations. The 19th century work is betrayed by the faces on the figures. They have a blandness of expression that is perfectly attuned to 19th century notions of piety. Victorian mediaevalism misses out on the intellectual strength of early gothic. What it

Victorian Gothic

expresses through its own art is a sentimental feeling that misrepresents the religious feeling of the past.

A key figure was D G Rossetti, an enthusiastic reader of several of Bulwer's novels. His mind may have been strange and unbalanced, but he did succeed in getting going a new aesthetic ideal with all the problems to which it gave rise. This was precisely his dream of the middle ages, which we must think of as resting in genuine understanding. This understanding stimulated a dream of the middle ages replacing religious experience by a mediaevalising charm. There is a huge difference between being charmed by pictures from an exotic past and adopting the beliefs that would have made those pictures meaningful.

Several efforts have been made to explain the connection of gothic with mystic illumination.

It can therefore be readily understood what determined the sudden change between 1140-1150, resulting in that wonderful accession of beauty to architectural design which we find in the Gothic. The incentive had to be a strong one, and of an eminently religious character, to accomplish the radical change of throwing over so absolutely the Norman, and commencing to build entirely on what are called Gothic lines. A careful examination of the proportions of the structures themselves, and the character of the decorations found in the finest examples of buildings representing that style, at once shows us that the incentive was the symbolism attached to the mysterious figure called the Vesica Piscis, which appears to be not only the principal feature upon which the whole style rests, but is also employed, as a symbol of the Divine, wherever we have Gothic Architecture, either in painted windows or mural decorations. Every Cathedral has its Vesica Piscis, often of enormous dimensions.

Geometry was synonymous with Masonry, and the very foundation of the Science of Geometry, as expounded by Euclid, was his first proposition. Every single problem in the whole of his books necessitates for its construction the use of this one foundation namely, "how to form an Equilateral Triangle," and this is the Mystical form of "the Knowledge of the Square." This triangle, symbolising the Logos, is therefore not only the beginning of the Science of Geometry, and therefore of Masonry, the Head of all the Sciences, but it is by that triangle that all Geometrical forms, and therefore forms of knowledge, are made, and it became the most mysterious and secret symbol of the Logos, for is it not written by St. John that "In the beginning was the Logos, and by it were all things made"; so the Vesica Piscis, the cradle of the Logos, became the great secret of Masonry, the foundation as we find it upon which Gothic Architecture was evolved, the means by which its wonderful plans were laid down, and the most reverenced figure in Religious Symbolism, as shown by its use in seals, engravings, sculptures, pictures, &c., throughout the Middle Ages. (Sidney Klein)

Victorian Gothic

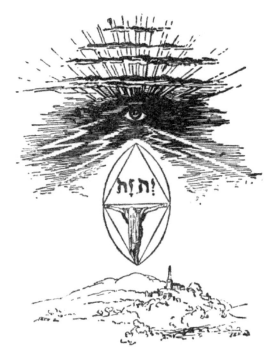

According to **Pankofksy** the gothic style was deliberately conceived as an embodiment of the mystical Christian neoplatonic wisdom of Dionysius and Eriugena:-

The light metaphysics of Eriugena looks forward to Grosseeste and Roger Bacon, and further ahead to Ficino.

Gothic style originated in the Abbey church of St Denis, just north of Paris under the inspiration and direction of **Abbe Suger** (1081-1151).

Suger wrote an autobiography and poetry. He had disagreements with St Bernard and with the austerity of the Cistercians. St Denis was identified with Dionysius the Areopagite whose pseudepigraphic

Victorian Gothic

writings inspired Eriugena 815 – c. 877 who in turn inspired the Kabbala and much else in the occult tradition.

For his remodelling of Knebworth in 1844 he employed architect **Henry Edward Kendall Jr** and for the interior decoration **John Dibblee Crace** from an old family firm, whose father had been a partner of Pugin. Nevertheless the whole scheme was essentially his own. With no wife around to restrain him, his fertile imagination had free play. The Bulls stood for Bulwer and the bats on barrels somehow represent Lytton.

The present unpopularity of Bulwer reflects the unpopularity of Victorian gothic for much of the twentieth century. St Pancras Station and the Midland Hotel was the building young architects were taught most to hate and most wished to knock down.

Literary Reputation

F R Leavis promoted the idea of *"the great tradition"* in his campaign for English Literature as a serious University subject. **Queenie Leavis** – his wife, collaborator and former pupil- wrote the following:-

"Lytton's inflated language means an inflation of sentiment, and his pseudo-philosophic nonsense and preposterous rhetoric carry with them inevitably a debasing of the novelist's currency. But they were taken seriously by the general public." - Fiction and the Reading Public, 1932

The Leavises, who dominated the university subject of English Literature for some years, had definite ideas on who were the greatest English novelists. It is not hard to find a critic with contemptuous opinions of one of their own idols. Here is Arthur Machen, Bulwer fan, occult novelist and member of the Golden Dawn:-

"a dull, industrious woman"
"we feel like a girls' school, compelled to listen to the 'now, young ladies' and the 'lessons' which every object on the road suggests."
"poor, dreary, draggle-tailed George Eliot"
"the works of George Eliot are the works of a superior insect—and nothing more." -Hieroglyphics 1902)

A R Orage found proto-Nietzschean ideas in the novels of Bulwer and Disraeli, but that did not restore his reputation. In some English critical quarters Nietzsche was no more popular than Bulwer. The snobbish Bloomsbury group were an anti-Nietzschean force. This is significant. What they put in his place was hardly intellectually satisfying, but that was not their aim. They have been compared to a Whig aristocracy. Theirs was the arrogant complacency of a class, surrounded with gratifying pleasures into which you get initiated. The ruling classes traditionally are uninterested in ideas. It is ideas that threaten to rob them of their privilege.

Literary Reputation

But time moves on and Bulwer has still not come back into his own. The disdain in which he is currently held should not be seen as entirely innocent. Some years ago I was introduced to an editor of Penguin Classics, to show him my proposal for publishing *Bulwer-Lytton's Last of the Barons*. I found him patronising and supercilious. He read my introduction, and his objection to my proposal was that "*I'm not sure where you are coming from*", presumably meaning he thought I was too right wing.

For years my wife had been telling me to read Charlotte Bronte's *Villette* and bought me the Penguin Classic edition, published not long after my meeting with that editor. The novel itself is superb, but having read the introduction I could see what he meant. This was obviously the sort of writing he wanted, full of modern morality and prejudice, fitting nineteenth century English literature into a comprehensively Marxist world view.

This doctrine justifies itself as enlightenment, on the model of the emancipation from superstition that got underway in the eighteenth century. Its arguments are rooted in assumptions about the moral imperative of equality. Even on that basis the position is hardly consistent, as it serves for a creed securing the status of an elite, a vehicle for the ambitions of those currently graduating from English literature courses in our universities, schooled in hectoring Marxist/feminist/postcolonial rhetoric.

Bulwer is not like that. He transports us into a different mindset, which is that of our ancestors, yet he rises above it. He is of his age but also beyond it, conscious of a higher more mysterious dimension.

Assessment

There is little point in trying to claim him as a great novelist. If that is what we are looking for we should go to the Russians, or sometimes the French. In comparison with Dostoyevsky or Proust, the works of English novelists are all flawed, though enough of them are fascinating. Bulwer can still have value for us. His responses to his own era could inspire ours to ours. He was an intellectual force, not just expressing attitudes of his age, but articulating the logic behind them, so important for understanding the Victorians and our own history.

Even if Bulwer's books are no longer read, that is a taste that could change. It is a bad mistake to think of him as unreadable.

He is classed by some sympathetic critics as a minor novelist, like his friend Disraeli, whom the Leavises did not despise, but it does not seem promising to promote him directly on that basis. Who today wants to read minor Victorian novelists? In his own time he was anything but minor. As a representative figure of his age he embodies a whole era with its values and strengths, as well as some weaknesses. There is permanent interest in that, but even more significant are his ideas, which are worth exploring for their own sake, and are not precisely mainstream. Interested in the man you will want to read his fiction for what he has to say, rather than comparing him unfavourably to Dickens, Thackeray or Eliot. The Victorians liked him; supposedly we do not, but subjects that occupied the Victorian public are of continuing concern. He offers more than just entertainment.

Focussing on him as an occult personality gives a dimension that transcends the historical. Themes connected with the occult are among the most interesting of the ideas developed in his novels. He is a figure around which revolve questions and inspirations which are still alive. The occult philosophy is not a dogma, not a faith, but something more like a creative vortex, which has delivered in the past and may do so again.

Appendix 1

The Gipsy Girl

ONCE more on foot, homewards. Time, sunset. 1824. Scene, the highway road, so curving as to be lost from sight at the distance of fifty yards, between a wood on one side, a broad patch of common sward on the other.

"Shall I tell you your fortune, my pretty young gentleman?"

The voice, young and silvery, startled me from my reverie, and by my side stood a gipsy girl. She was so handsome! The most beautiful specimen I have ever seen of a race often beautiful in youth.

"Pray do!" said I, and I crossed her small palm with silver. "Only pray, give me a sweetheart half as pretty as yourself."

The girl was, no doubt, used to such compliments, but she blushed as if new to them. She looked me in the face, quickly but searchingly, and then bent her dark eyes over my hand.

"Chut! chut!" she said with a sound of sorrowful pity, " but you have known sorrows already. You lost your father when you were very young. You have brothers, but no sister. Ah! you have had a sweetheart when you were a mere boy. You will never see her again, never. The line is clean broken off. It cut you to the heart. You nearly died of it. You have conquered, but you'll never be as gay again."

I snatched away my hand in amaze.

"You are indeed a witch!" said I, falteringly.

"Did I offend you? I'll not say any more of what has passed ; let me look for your good-luck in the time to come."

"Do so, and say something pleasant. Conceal the bad fortune as much as you can."

I felt very credulous and superstitious.

"Chut! chut! but that new star thwarts you much."

"What new star?"

"I don't know what they call it. But it makes men fond of strange studies, and brings about crosses and sorrows that you never think to have. Still, you are a prosperous gentleman, you will never come to want, you will be much before the world and raise your head high, but I fear you'll not have the honours you count on now. Chut! chut! pity! pity! you'll know scandal and slander, you'll be spoken ill of where you least deserve. That will vex you much, but you are proud and will not stoop to show it. Your best friends and your worst enemies will be women. You'll hunger for love all your life, and you will have much of it, but less satisfaction than sorrow. Chut! chut! how often you will be your own enemy ! but don't be down-hearted, there is plenty of good fortune and success in store for you not like me. Look at my hand. See here, where the cross comes against the line of life! "

"What does that mean?"

134

Appendix 1

"Sorrow and it is very near!"

"Nay, you don't believe for yourself all that you say to others. Our fortunes are not written in the palm of our hands."

"For those who can read them yes," said the gipsy. "But very few have the gift. Some can read fortunes by fixing their eyes on anything the gift comes to them."

I don't pretend to give the exact words of the girl. They were spoken quickly, and often in florid phrases, but, to the best of my recollection, I repeat the substance. We continued to walk on, and talk; we became familiar, and she interested me greatly. I questioned her as to the women of her caste, their mode of life, their religion, their origin, their language. Her replies were evasive, and often enigmatical. I remember that she said there were but two genuine clans of gipsies in England, and that the one bore the generic name of Fahey, the other of Smith, from the names their first dukes or leaders bore. She said that many of their traditions as to their origin and belief were dying out that some of them had become what she called Christians, though, from her account, it was but a heathen sort of Christianity. She took great pains to convince me that they were not wilful impostors in their belief that they could predict the future. I have since learned that though they placed great faith in the starry influences, their ideas were quite distinct from the astrology known to us. Nor was their way of reading the lines in the hand at all like that described in books of chiromancy.

From these subjects we passed on to others more tender and sentimental. The girl seemed to have taken a liking to me, but she was coy and modest.

"I should much like," said I, abruptly, "to pass a few days with you and your tribe. Do you think I might? "

The young gipsy's eyes brightened vividly.

"That I am sure you can, if you can put up with it the like of you, a real born gentleman. Grandmother does as she will with the men, and I have my own way with her. Oh, do stay! Stop I don't see that in the lines in my hand I only see the cross."

I could not help kissing the little hand. She would not let me kiss the lips, which were pursed up in pretty, wistful doubt.

By-and-by, on a broader patch of the common land, and backed by a deeper mass of the woods, I saw before me the gipsy encampment. Just then the sun set. The clouds around it red and purple, the rest of the sky clear and blue, and Venus, the love star, newly risen.

We passed by some ragged, swarthy children lolling on the grass; they rose and followed us. Three young men, standing round an older gipsy, who was employed in tinkering, stared at me somewhat fiercely. But the girl took me by the hand and led me into the spacious tent. A woman, apparently of great age, sate bending over a wood fire, on which boiled a huge pot. To this woman my young companion spoke low and eagerly, in a language at which I could not guess my way to a word the old woman looking hard at me all the time, and shaking her head at first in dissent, but gradually she

Appendix 1

seemed talked into acquiescence. The dear
little gipsy, indeed, seemed to me irresistible,
the tones of her voice were so earnest yet so
coaxing. At length she turned round to me and
said joyfully:

"You are welcome to stay as long as you
like. But stop what money have you got
about you?"

I felt as if an illusion was gone. It went to
my heart to hear the girl refer to money. Was
her kindness, then, all sordid? Was I to buy
the hospitable rites proffered to me?

I replied very coldly, that I had enough
money to pay for any civilities I might receive.

The girl's face flushed, and her eyes sparkled angrily.

"You mistake me. I did not think you
could. I spoke for your safety. It may be
dangerous to have money. Give it all to grandmother's care. She will return it to you, untouched, when you leave us."

With an inexpressible feeling of relief and
trust, I instantly drew forth all the coins about
me and gave it to the old woman,
who took what must have seemed to her a large
sum without showing any emotion, and slid it
into her pocket.

"You don't think I shall let you lose a
sixpence? "said the girl, drawing up her stature
proudly.

"Oh, no! I wish it were thousands."

Poor child! At these words the pride
vanished, her eyes moistened.

Then the old woman rose and took some
embers from the fire, and strewed them on the
ground, and bade me stand in them. She said
something to the girl, who went forth and
called in all the other gipsies men, women and
children. There were about a dozen of them
altogether. As soon as they were assembled the
old woman, taking my right hand in hers, and
pointing to the embers beneath my feet, began
to address them in the gipsy tongue. They
all stood listening reverently. When she had
finished they bowed their heads, came up to me,
and by word and sign made me understand that

I was free of the gipsy tent, and welcome to the
gipsy cheer.

Resolved to make myself popular, I exerted
all my powers to be lively and amusing hail
fellow, well me ! The gipsies said little themselves, but they seemed to enjoy my flow of talk
and my high spirits. We all sate round the great
fire a primitive oriental group. By-and-by
the pot was taken off, and its contents distributed
amongst us ; potatoes and bread, fragments of
meat stewed to rags, and seasoned with herbs of
a taste before unknown to me. Altogether I
thought the podrida excellent.

The old crone, who seemed the Queen of the
camp, did not, however, partake of this mess.
She had a little dish of her own broiled on the
embers, of odd, uncouth form. I did not like
to be too inquisitive that night, but I learned
from my young patroness the next day, that her
grandmother was faithful to the customs of the
primitive gipsies, and would eat nothing in the

Appendix 1

shape of animal food that had not died a natural death. Her supper had been a broiled hedgehog found in a trap.

I spent with these swarthy wanderers five or six very happy days, only alloyed by the fear that I should be called on to requite the hospitality I received by participating in some theft upon poultry-yard or drying-ground, that would subject me to the tread-mill. Had I been asked, I very much doubt if I should have had the virtue to refuse. However, the temptation, luckily, was never pressed upon me, nor did I witness anything to justify the general suspicion of gipsy errors as to the meum and tuum.

Once only a fine goose, emerging from the pot, inflamed my appetite and disturbed my conscience. The men generally absented them-selves from the camp at morning, together with a donkey and their tinkering apparatus, some-times returning at noon, sometimes not till night.

The women went about fortune-telling, the children watched on the common for any stray passenger whom they might induce to enter the camp and cross with silver the hand of the oracle, for the old woman sate by the fire all day. My young gipsy went forth by herself also on pretence of telling fortunes, but we had fixed a spot on the road at which I always joined her, and we used then to wander through the green lanes, or sit on some grassy bank, talking to each other with open hearts.

I think that the poor girl felt for me, not exactly love, but that sort of wild, innocent fondness a young Indian savage might feel for the first fair face from Europe that had ever excited her wonder. Once the instinctive greed of her caste seized her at the sight of a young horseman; and she sprang from my side to run after him, not resting till he had slipped from his horse, crossed her hand, and heard his fortunes.

When she came back to my side she showed me half-a-crown with such glee! I turned away coldly, and walked off. She stood rooted to the spot for a moment, and then ran after me and threw her arms round my neck.

"Are you angry?"

"Angry, no, but to run after that young man"

"Jealous? oh, I'm so happy! then you do care for me."

As if with a sudden impulse, she raised herself on tiptoe, clung to me, and kissed my forehead. I clasped her in my arms, but she glided from them like a serpent, and ran off, back to the encampment, as if afraid of me and of herself.

One morning she was unusually silent and reserved. I asked her, reproachfully, why she was so cold.

"Tell me," she said abruptly, "tell me truly, do you love me?"

"I do indeed." And so I thought.

"Will you marry me, then?"

"Marry you?" I cried, aghast. "Marry? Alas! I would not deceive you that is impossible."

137

Appendix 1

*"I don't mean," cried she impetuously, but
not seeming hurt at my refusal, "I don't mean
as you mean marriage according to your
fashion. I never thought of that, but marry me
as we marry."*

"How is that?"

*"You will break a piece of burned earth
with me a tile, for instance into two halves."*

"Well?"

*"In grandmother's presence. That will be
marriage. It lasts only five years. It is not
long," she said pleadingly.*

*"And if you want to leave me before, how
could I stay you?"*

*Poor dear child! for child after all she was,
in years and in mind; how charming she looked
then! Alas! I went further for a wife and
fared worse.*

Two days after this proposition, I lost sight
`of her for ever.`

Appendix 2

Bulwer-Lytton

by

John S Moore

Visit Knebworth, ancestral home of the Lytton family, and before the first Baron's writing desk the guide informs you that although he was a very famous novelist in his day nobody reads him any more. This is not much of an exaggeration. The last of his books to be popular was *The Last Days of Pompeii*, a cruder work than his best historical novels, though credited with inspiring Madame Blavatsky to her adventurous career as mystical hierophant and founder of the theosophical society. But it would be wrong to conclude from the fact that he is not read to the judgement that he is not worth reading. Why has this idea taken hold?

Born Edward Bulwer in 1803, he was educated at Trinity College Cambridge. He began writing to finance an extravagant lifestyle as man of fashion. He was Secretary of State for the Colonies in 1858. For his achievements as novelist, playwright and statesman, he was elevated to the peerage in 1866. For forty years he was known as Bulwer, for twenty-two, having added his mother's surname on inheriting Knebworth, Bulwer-Lytton, and the last seven as Lord Lytton. He died in 1873.

Lytton's work expresses some of the most significant intellectual currents of the nineteenth century, several of which are far from are exhausted. He treated intelligently and interestingly perennial themes of good and evil, of freedom and despotism, egoism and altruism, life affirmation and the power of will. His treatment can seem all the fresher partly because he is no longer familiar. His influence was world-wide. It was notable in Germany, whose deep and thoughtful culture he both affected and was affected by. He was influenced by Schiller (whom he translated), and by Goethe, sharing something

Appendix 2

of the latter's eclectic liveliness, and exploring subjects that strongly suggest his speculations about the daemonic. His novel of thirteenth century Italy, *Rienzi*, inspired Wagner's third opera.

Britain and Germany have often seemed far apart culturally, looking to different types of philosophy, and separated by a degree of mutual contempt. British writers deplore Germany's tendency to obscurity and dangerously misguided enthusiasm, Germans British pedestrianism of ideas and arrogant insularity. To some continental critics, the stranglehold of the old universities has adversely affected the whole of English cultural life. Such criticism was by no means unechoed in Britain.. Some of Bulwer's thoughts upon power and charisma suggest a discontent that a complacent English culture has often felt able to dismiss as typical of an alien tradition.

Coleridge and Carlyle are examples of that enthusiasm for Germany that was a significant strand in nineteenth century British culture. Many in Victorian times had ideas of Germany as a kind of alternative England, a place of new possibilities, romantically rich, a new country to be constructed. We may think of the creation of an original German culture as an international project, with a not altogether happy outcome. Viewing Bulwer as part of this is to guard against thinking solely in terms of English literature. For the German connection see ZIPSER Richard A., *Edward Bulwer-Lytton and Germany,*: Berne & Frankfurt/M.: Herbert Lang, 1974.

Allan Conrad Christensen, author of one modern study (*Edward Bulwer-Lytton, the fiction of new regions*, Athens, GA University of Georgia Press 1976), asserts that Lytton was "*not one of the very great novelists*" and that he is interesting for his ideals and aspirations more than for the perfection of his work. He says that he throws valuable light on the thought of the Victorians, on their view of the world. Though he also argues for his intrinsic interest, many might think that Bulwer is mostly of concern to historians, and students of the Victorian age, and that for literature we should read other novelists. That he was original and influential no one would deny. Others have surpassed him in some, perhaps most, of the genres in which he worked. *Vanity Fair* has been called the masterpiece of the fashionable, *Oliver Twist* of the Newgate school. Some conclude that his influence has passed on, into other and greater writers, with the implicit suggestion that he has nothing to say to us. This is very disputable, certainly in view of much of the nineteenth literature that still continues to be read. Many of the ideas expressed are as lively and relevant today as they were when he wrote.

As for Bulwer's deficiency in purely literary qualities, that is less decisive than some critics have held. Understanding something of what his ideas are, we no longer judge him by some simplistic canon of what is or is not "great literature". Supposed weaknesses of style like his unfashionable archaism, need not obstruct appreciation. Admittedly he has acquired an unfortunate reputation for corniness. The opening lines of his *Paul Clifford* (1830) have inspired a number of childish jokes, largely through the influence of Schultz's *Peanuts* strip cartoon. The sentence runs: - *"It was a dark and stormy night and the rain fell in torrents--except at occasional intervals, when it was checked by a violent gust of wind which swept up the streets (for it is in London that our scene lies), rattling along the housetops, and fiercely agitating the scanty flame of the lamps that struggled against the darkness."* This is supposed to be so laughable that someone is offering an annual 'Bulwer-Lytton prize' for bad writing.

Another obvious obstacle is the sheer diversity and range of his work. No one is likely to be drawn to

Appendix 2

all of it. I only feel qualified to argue for the interest of some of it, and to indicate a few of his more notable themes. Far from being superseded, his best work is unique in English literature, of permanent interest, and quite unfairly ignored. It would be surprising if someone who made so many successful hits never attained to lasting originality Admittedly the idea of having to plough through his whole oeuvre would be dismaying. I am prepared to concede that a work like *Ernest Maltravers* (1837)* may well be dead for the rest of time, though I would not want to pontificate on the subject. Who could say where a Lytton revival might lead?

We can certainly see him as a representative Victorian, with his roots appropriately in an earlier era. He was a survivor from the days of George IV. His first poetry was published in 1820, his first novel in 1827. All his life he cultivated a image which came to seem worse than old fashioned. It inspired counter accusations of effeminacy from Tennyson, whom he had himself accused of girlishness. This inspired a lifelong feud.

The young Bulwer, who began as an admirer of Byron, found a new hero in Bentham, entering parliament in the reform interest in 1831. At this period he wrote of the need to balance the urge to self fulfilment with more social concerns. His *Pelham* (1828) allegedly changed the fashion from Byronism to the moral earnestness of the Victorian social reformers. For amoral individualism, the Byronism of the 1820s had prefigured the Nietzscheanism of the end of the century. After the 1820s people tired of egoistic assertion for a season, much as, following a similar reaction, was to happen with Nietzsche. Bulwer found fertile material in the dialectic of egoism and idealism. The tension between the two suggests what Aleister Crowley, the prophet of Magick and Thelema, and admirer of Lytton's work, said of the conflict between his own Beast personality and his utopian, Shelleyan side, though in his case it

142

might all reduce to egoism. He remarks on Zanoni's sacrifice in language that time has not softened into respectability.

"We have a sentimental idea of self sacrifice, the kind which is most esteemed by the vulgar and is the essence of popular Christianity. It is the sacrifice of the strong to the weak. This is wholly against the principles of evolution. Any nation which does this systematically on a sufficiently large scale destroys itself. The sacrifice is vain, the weak are not even saved. Consider the action of Zanoni in going to the scaffold in order to save his silly wife. The gesture was magnificent; it was evidence of his own supreme courage and moral strength; but if every one acted on that principle the race would deteriorate and disappear".

With the reaction against rationalism and a new cultural climate, Bulwer's lifelong occult interests gained a new relevance. He was a living link between the original Romantic Movement, and the belief in the power of the imagination that characterised the aesthetic revolt. His conception of the ideal world and the soul prefigured the principles of the symbolists and decadents who made up romanticism's second wind. The symbolist movement was largely underpinned by occult philosophy. Mystery was intrinsic to the reaction against the supposed rationality of the high Victorians. Bulwer had a rich and genuine occult learning that earned him the respect of all the leading figures of the occult revival. He had made an intensive study of magical writers like Iamblichus, Psellus, and Cornelius Agrippa, and was not above claiming secret knowledge and initiation into the Rosicrucian brotherhood.

The concern with egoism led to a preoccupation with villainy. In defence of the subject matter of his Newgate novels, Bulwer argued that crime reveals deep truth about human nature. This was another of his seminal ideas. Arabaces the magician in *The Last Days of Pompeii* (1834), last

Appendix 2

descendant of the Egyptian royal line, is a gloomy, sensual aristocratic criminal. The theme was more deeply explored in his occult stories. In *The Haunted and the Haunters*† (1857), he presents a malevolent character who transcends the Byronic to create a fascinating image of daemonic will. In the full version of the story, he is encountered in his contemporary embodiment as Richards, the mysterious long-lived being responsible for the hauntings. Sometimes described as the best ghost story ever written, this is arguably his masterpiece. He cut it short in later editions, because he wanted to develop the theme into a full-length novel. It became *A Strange Story* (1862), where the same malignant will is personified as Margrave, an evil character who wants to live forever. This desire comes across as a powerful image of life affirmation, though in the form of black magic.

White magic is portrayed in the earlier *Zanoni* (1842). Zanoni stands for the virtuous version of daemonic will. He has lived for many centuries as a member of a wise circle of initiates who have discovered the secret of eternal life. Taking another's place on the scaffold, during the Reign of Terror, he offered the pattern for Sidney Carton's sacrifice in Dickens's *A Tale of Two Cities*. Lytton stated that this novel represents the fullest expression of his thought. We can think of it as a Rosicrucian novel of ideas. It brought to a nineteenth century audience the timelessly fascinating Rosicrucian alchemical tradition. The character of Zanoni represents his synthesis of these ideals. For its treatment of these, it belongs with his historical novels.

Late in his career, Bulwer turned against the pretensions of scientific rationalism, expressing hostility towards Marxism, Darwinism and socialist utopias. Other of his contemporaries expressed comparable reservations, not least Tennyson, whose *Locksley Hall Sixty Years After* shows his discontent with the ideals of progress he had done so much to hymn. *The Coming Race*

Appendix 2

(1873) has sometimes been interpreted as one of the earliest blasts in a dystopic tradition that was to culminate in Orwell's *1984* and Huxley's *Brave New World*, books which for a few decades offered powerful prophylactics against some disturbing modern tendencies.

How much his thoughts on will derived from philosophical sources like Schopenhauer, if at all, and how much from humbler sources like Balzac, has been a subject of argument.

Whatever his inspiration there are fertile possibilities in the subject. *The Coming Race* explores some of them in the form of science fiction. Vril is will power made into the direct energy source of society. (The word survives on the supermarket shelf as Bovril). Like Huxley's *Brave New World,* the novel included speculations about interesting technological developments, but set in the framework of an inhuman and unacceptable future. The scientific perfection of this society is that of another species, and really intolerable to the human being.

High claims have been made for this book, and even for the idea of vril, which has been described as anticipating nuclear energy. As science fiction it long predated Wells who was impressed by it,

His idea of historical romance is outlined in his introduction to *Harold, or the Last of the Saxon Kings* (1848), serious history mixed with romance. This offers a natural framework for such themes as the perils of a political career, and the meaning of aristocracy, subjects unfortunately prone to easy trivialisation. The historical novel itself is a genre that has sometimes been degraded to the level of feminine emotional pornography. With the debased romanticism of *"romantic fiction"* the aristocratic ideal becomes little more than a form of titillation for female readers. So the seriousness and originality of Bulwer's treatment may be overlooked. The eras he writes about he chooses

Appendix 2

not just for their dramatic interest. At his best he was writing historical novels of ideas. *The Last Days of Pompeii*, for all its merits, has presumably had its day. Brilliant entertainment for its time, its concessions to popular sentiment give an inadequate image of his powers. Modern readers who want that sort of thing seem to prefer Robert Graves's evocations of the Roman Empire in his Claudius series. *Pompeii* gives some intriguing insights into the Victorian imagination. But the interest of *Rienzi* (1835), and *The Last of the Barons* (1843) goes much further. In these novels, important universal issues are treated, unresolved arguments aired.

Bulwer teaches a history that deserves to be better known, bringing it imaginatively alive, and revealing a lot about nineteenth century British attitudes towards it. *Rienzi* expresses something of his social radicalism. It anticipates the intellectual atmosphere that generated fascism in its engrossing concern with charisma, the nature of

political leadership, nationalism and ambition. He says that the Roman people rejected Rienzi's leadership because they were not worthy of him. He holds that it was the same with the English who rejected Cromwell's republic. His description of Charles II, as "*the lewd pensioner of Louis*", reveals something of his political position. The aristocratic families of the Orsini and the Colonna come across as negative and destructive forces, though their point of view is by no means presented without sympathy.

The Last of the Barons was his next novel after *Zanoni*. Most critics acknowledge it to be one of his best. Perhaps we can trace a link with the heroic theme of its predecessor. Much as Zanoni is a hero held up for our admiration, it could be argued that Richard Neville, Earl of Warwick, known as the Kingmaker, represents his ideal in a more earthly form. This is nobility benevolent and not simply Byronic. He based his writing on a thorough study of contemporary sources, including

146

Appendix 2

the chroniclers like Hall, that Shakespeare read for his tetralogy on the Wars of the Roses. This epoch was England at its most self absorbed, the time when English literature retreated north of the border and perpendicular architecture developed in virtual isolation from continental influences. Perhaps such history is not of world-wide interest; its concerns reflect deep into the essence of English nationhood. Bulwer has an intriguing thesis that Warwick the Kingmaker had a better vision of England than did Edward IV and his Tudor successors. It cannot be said that the thesis obtrudes. We are hardly aware of it till the end of the book. Viewpoints of other, often opposed, characters are treated very sympathetically. The novel may even at first seem to be about the rise of the new middle classes, with heroes like Nicholas Alwyn, the ambitious goldsmith, and Master Warner, the inventor, who looks back to Friar Bacon and forward to the industrial revolution. Warwick is far from a mere apologist for the power of exploiters. Far more than the old order,

he represents England in all its contradictions. Considerations of policy are always tempered by a deep sense of traditional liberties. The value of aristocracy becomes apparent where liberty is overridden in the name of reform.

In this feudal vision is a wonderful lost cause to compare with Jacobitism. As a lost cause it could even have more appeal than that of the Stuarts, who might be perceived as primarily a Scottish dynasty. Bulwer links it with his own pride of ancestry; one of his own ancestors is periodically mentioned throughout the book as fighting on the Lancastrian side. The value of lost causes has often been understood as far more than that of doomed classes or misfit individuals. Even in their failure they are somehow liberating, a challenge to the idea that justice lies with the victors. The eighteenth century Whig settlement with its all embracing claim to represent freedom and reason was confronted by an alternative. The defeated cause, especially after 1745, inspired the most

Appendix 2

romantic emotions, as captured in Lady Nairne's beautiful songs. This book does something the same for the equally well known Tudor settlement.

In the very notion of the lost cause there is a world of emotional possibilities to enrich the present. A settlement that is found oppressive may be countered by this spirit. We live in a world in which a number of cultures and countries have recently experienced defeat. In a demoralised culture, it is important to find some compensation for defeat. Factors such as material wealth and erotic enjoyment generally offer consolation. What is most oppressive is that we are told that what we experience as defeat is not defeat, that it is really a triumph we are simply too backward to understand. We are under pressure to think what the dominant group in society means us to think, confounding power with wisdom. Despite the occasional encouragement when dissenting points of view find their way into the newspapers, it is hard for such attitudes to sustain themselves.

Bombarded with orthodox propaganda, it is hard to reject what we feel we ought to reject. How can we resist the idea that we live among reasonable people worthy of respect?

That other values than those in authority live and flourish within our society goes without saying, but typically their official status is low, and they are derided as outmoded, or unenlightened. Those who live by them are under pressure to change. Theirs is denied to be a perspective from which much develops. Against this tyranny art can operate as a subversive force. As a way of memory and of crystallisation, it opens the gate to enjoyment that is otherwise barred. Artists and writers create separate worlds where it is possible to ignore the pressure of outside opinion. *The Last of the Barons* is such a work. As a novel of a lost cause, preserving as literature Warwick's vision of aristocracy based on popular affection, lies much of its aesthetic value. In this sense we can see the book as successful and satisfying, the creation of a

Appendix 2

self-contained other world where ideas and values do not keep changing into one another.

Even as a historical novelist Bulwer-Lytton is universally held to be inferior to such masters as Hugo, Dickens and Scott, presumably as regards character, psychological drama, and other pure literary qualities. But he has a different sort of interest. He participates in the intellectual climate in a different way. He was writing a different sort of novel, whose interest is largely in its ideas. I strongly deny that his books have lost their relevance. They maintain interesting historical theses. It is recognised that the *Last of the Barons* is more historically accurate than Scott's novels, certainly than his English ones. Bulwer's historical research was deep and thorough. But even Scott is little read now.

One thesis is that the mediaeval barons were the foundation of English liberty. Even by Warwick's day, as Bulwer points out, they were still half Norman. He puts forward an argument for the value of feudalism, contending that English liberty grew out of the feudal past, the Norman freedom of the barons, their history and traditions. These values were to lay dormant for 150 years to re-emerge in the Cromwellian republic. This view is an alternative to the Saxonism that is emphasised in *Harold*, and sits more easily with the cosmopolitanism of the post war era. Feudalism involves voluntary commitment to rightful authority. Against this was the new monarchical absolutism with its basis in Machiavelli, appealing to the thrusting new middle class, and promoted by Edward IV, Richard III and the Tudors. Bulwer presents the young Duke of Gloucester, the future Richard III, as a serious student of these new ideas. Not only is he intelligent, ruthless and brave, as Shakespeare portrays him, but also a more sympathetic character, in his own way an idealist rather than a mere villain.

Appendix 2

Machiavelli represents rationalisation. We may think of him as a revolutionary, the Marx or Lenin of his day. One dispenses with morality for the duration of the revolution; after that it is presumably to return. Machiavellianism means cynicism about power and about the immovable beliefs of the people, to which hypocrisy has to be paid as tribute. Some basic questions of political philosophy present themselves. How much can a society be based upon true beliefs? There is a dialogue with Shakespeare, especially on the character of Gloucester, the significance of Machiavelli and the merits of the Tudor despotism. We see how much Shakespeare was writing Tudor propaganda.

There are various sub themes that might have some contemporary resonance. The descriptions of the court of Edward IV in the Tower of London reveal much about nineteenth century ideas of effeminacy. Despite Edward's military prowess and somewhat brutal courage when called upon, he presides over a frivolous feminine culture, preoccupied with fashion, entertainment and display. Another theme is the political use made of hypocritical piety. Another is that of the newly created aristocrats, represented by Hastings, relatives of the Queen, pitted against the old baronage in the effort to undermine its power. And it is instructive to see Warwick as putting Edward IV in power then regretting what he had done.

Today, when England is looking for a new identity, it is worth looking at earlier settlements. For this reason alone *The Last of the Barons* would be worth rereading. Even for making modern points, it can be useful to focus on something from history. There is much in national life that is only tolerable once we have risen to a vision, one might call it illusion, of mutual agreement. Where there are few we can agree with completely, politics becomes a matter of alliances. To be against something can give a feeling of unity, though our individual voices are unheard.

Appendix 2

The unifying cause here is regret at the triumph of a modernising despotism. Here is a vision of England in one of its most formative eras, as engaging and thought provoking as much of Shakespeare.

New Labour's reforms seem likely to create a nostalgia for the things it is setting out to destroy. Most obvious of these is the vestigial political power of the old hereditary nobility. Encouraged by this attack, new voices are raised against the monarchy. Soon the nation itself may be called upon to give up its sovereignty to join a new European federation. Also some people are talking about the crisis of English identity as Scotland and Wales make moves away from the union, and the Union Jack is decried as a racist symbol. There is potential solace in the England before the Tudors, and a lament for freedoms and values that went into eclipse. This is not jingoism. There is little imperialism in *The Last of the Barons*, unless against the French who are still regarded as fair game. And it is a perfectly readable book, certainly as much so as much of what is still published in popular paperback editions and expected to be taken seriously as great literature. Much of its merit is its intellectual content. It is meaty enough in this respect. Also it evokes a believable picture of a unique, complex and little known era, and compelling psychological portraits of interesting historical characters. There are riches for which there is no space in this introduction. It is hard to think of any significant feature of the period that has been altogether omitted.

Until recently the motive for this journey into the roots of English national feeling and identity would have been generally obvious. The former is increasingly marginalised to the frivolity of football and out of the way places like Northern Ireland. In some quarters it is so unfashionable as to have become almost incomprehensible. In others it is identified with a narrow party line.

Appendix 2

Historical understanding is obscured by the moralistic prejudices of right and left. *The Last of the Barons* is good enough to bear a new interpretation. This well constructed book with its far from happy ending can speak a new message as much of the mere background becomes a source of illumination to a generation that is forgetting what once was common currency. It relates to a traditional image and interpretation of England that has played a large role in history and if only for this reason would be worth remembering.

Enthusiasts for reform may be tempted to dismiss the whole idea of such an artistic value as mere right wing tosh. In one sense, of course, romanticising the lost cause is inevitably a reactionary idea. But that is not exactly the point that is being made. The object is not directly political, it speaks more to frustration of the will, disillusion and disgust with politics. For aesthetic purposes the lost cause is often far more valuable than the live political option. With the revolt against a one-sided, often philistine, rationalism, comes restoration of imaginative balance. A vision, even a fantasy, of historical rootedness offers an antidote to the rootless metropolitanism of an obnoxious zeitgeist. Such a counteragent is not necessarily rightist, unless as conflicting with certain current loyalties, self righteously assured of their unimpeachable rationality.

John S Moore 1998

- With respect to Ernest Maltravers, I have been put right by Frank O'Donoghue, who unlike me has read the book and tells me it is excellent.

-

Fri, 27 Nov 1998 20:33:44 -0000

From: "Frank" To: me

Appendix 2

Dear John

I was interested to read your Bulwer-Lytton piece on your website but I must take issue with your opinion of

Ernest Maltravers. Do you include Alice, or the Mysteries in the same category? As you may have gathered these are two (one?) of my favourite works and I am hoping you are not basing your opinion on a thorough reading.

I hope I don't sound over-critical; apologies, if I do because the piece was generally good.

Can you recommend any other sources of information on EGBL and his works?

Thank you for your time.

Frank O'Donoghue

Subject:

Re: EGBL

Date:

Sat, 28 Nov 1998 23:30:02 +0000

From: me To: Frank

Mea culpa. I have not read Ernest Maltravers. I should remedy this. My remark about it is mostly based on a negative report from one of my friends. I do not mean to disparage any of Lytton's work, only to argue for the merits of what I enjoy, which is most of what I have read of him, and to understand why he has fallen into such oblivion. I confess to a possibly irrational prejudice against reading the whole oeuvre. Your own opinion is a fact of which I must take account. As for material on Bulwer-Lytton, the Internet you can explore as well as I can. I searched the British Library catalogues, and read a few books and

Appendix 2

articles there, including Christensen and Zipser, an interesting monograph by Liljegren, Bulwer-Lytton and Isis Unveiled, & dipped into the multi volume biographies by his son and his grandson. I would like to bring out a new edition of The Last of the Barons. I spoke to the editor of Penguin Classics about this, and though he seemed to think it might be a good idea, he was discouraging as people like that usually are.

Date:

Mon, 30 Nov 1998 20:44:06 -0000

From: "Frank" To: me

John

Thank you for your recent e-mail regarding Ernest Maltravers.

I am pleased that I was right about you not having read the book. I don't have a TV myself but it would make (together with Alice) a marvellous costume drama; I cannot praise the books too highly.

If you do get around to reading them, I'd be very interested in your opinions.

Regards

Frank

PS. My interest in EGBL was sparked by Wagner's mentions of his works in Mein Leben.

April 2018-04-20

Appendix 2

I still have not read *Ernest Maltravers*, but I did read *Alice or the Mysteries*. It is excellent. The only flaw is that it does seem to presuppose a reading of the earlier novel.

Appendix 3

This paper was presented as part of Bulwer's bicentennial celebration at Knebworth House on 23rd May 2003

**Bulwer-Lytton's Harold
(Everything is will)**

From *Harold* (1848)

Hilda gazed on the hideous form before her; and so had her soul fallen from its arrogant pride of place, that instead of the scorn with which so foul a pretender to the Great Art had before inspired the King-born Prophetess, her veins tingled with credulous awe.
"Art thou a mortal like myself," she said after a pause, "or one of those beings often seen by the shepherd in mist and rain, driving before them their shadowy flocks? one of those of whom no man knoweth whether they are of earth or of Helheim ? whether they have ever known the lot and conditions of flesh, or are but some dismal race between body and spirit, hateful alike to gods and to men ?"
The dreadful hag shook her head, as if refusing to answer the question, and said,
"Sit we down, sit we down by the dead dull pool, and if thou wouldst be wise as I am, wake up all thy wrongs, fill thyself with hate, and let thy thoughts be curses. Nothing is strong on earth but the Will; and hate to the will is as the iron in the hands of the war-man."
"Ha!" answered Hilda, "then thou art indeed one of the loathsome brood whose magic is born, not of the aspiring soul, but of the fiendlike heart. And between us there is no union. I am of the race of those of whom priests and kings reverenced and honoured as the oracles of Heaven; and rather let my lore be dimmed and weakened, in admitting the humanities of hope
and love, than be lightened by the glare of the wrath that Lok and Rana bear the children of men."
"What, art thou so base and so doting," said the hag, with fierce contempt", as to know that another has supplanted thine Edith, that all the schemes of thy life are undone, and yet feel no hate for the man who bath wronged her and thee? -the man who had never been king if thou hadst not breathed into him the ambition of rule ? Think, and curse! "
"My curse would wither the heart that is entwined within his," answered Hilda; "and," she added abruptly, as if eager to escape from her own impulses, "didst thou not tell- me, even now, that the wrong would be redressed, and his betrothed yet be his bride on the appointed day?"
" Ha ! home, then!-home! and weave the charmed woof of the banner, broider it with zimmes and with gold worthy the standard of a king; for I tell thee, that where that banner is planted, shall Edith clasp with bridal arms her adored. And the hwata thou hast read by the bautastein, and in the temple of the Briton's revengeful gods, shall be fulfilled."
" Dark daughter of Hela," said the Prophetess, "whether demon or god hath inspired thee, I hear in my spirit a voice, that tells me thou hast pierced to a truth that my lore could not reach. Thou art houseless and poor; I will give wealth "to thine age if thou wilt stand with me by the altar of Thor, .and let thy galdra unriddle the secrets that have baffled mine Own. All foreshown to me hath ever come to pass, but in a sense other than that in which my soul read the rune and the dream, the leaf and the fount, the star and the Scin-laeca. My husband slain in his youth; my daughter maddened with woe; her lord murdered on his hearthstone; Sweyn, whom I loved as my child," -the Vala paused, contending against her own emotions,-" I loved them all," she faltered, clasping her hands, " for them I tasked the future. The future promised fair; I lured them to their doom, and when the doom came, !the promise was kept ! but how? -and now, Edith, the

156

Appendix 3

*last of my race; Harold, the pride of my pride !-speak,
thing of Horror and Night, canst thou disentangle the
web in which my soul struggles, weak as the fly in the
spider's mesh ? "*

*. "On the third night from this, will I stand with thee
by the altar of Thor, and unriddle the rede of my
masters, unknown and unguest, whom thou hadst
duteously served. And ere the sun rise, the greatest
mystery earth knows shall be bare to thy soul ! "*

*- As the witch spoke, a cloud passed over the moon;
and before the light broke forth again, the hag had
vanished. There was only seen in the dull pool, the
water-rat swimming through the rank sedges ; only in
the forest, the grey wings of owl, fluttering heavily
across the glades ; only in the grass, red eyes of the
bloated toad.*

Harold is far from Lytton's best historical novel. I have
to qualify that statement by saying that is only my own
opinion, because there are some who disagree. To my
taste it is nowhere near as good as *Rienzi*, or *The Last
of the Barons*. As one critic has said Bulwer rationalises
away much of the wonder and strangeness of the
period. The above eve of battle passage reminds all too
obviously of Shakespeare's weird sisters. Nevertheless,
it is worth a closer look..

A modern reader might not see much beyond the worn
cliché of the wicked witch, with an evil philosophy of
hatred . "Nothing is strong on earth but will" suggests
comic strip Nazis and of a loveless un-christian creed of
black magic. *Triumph of the Will* was the famous Nazi
film. However, Bulwer's attitude is very far from a
straightforward condemnation of such a view of the
will, or mere Christian abhorrence. The witch's
statement does not represent an unreservedly
villainous attitude to be condemned. Bulwer was
himself very interested in magic of a most ambitious
kind. His association with the famous French magician
Eliphas Levi is well known. Levi praised Bulwer in the
highest terms, and his own 'astral light' is thought to
have influenced the idea of the vril force in *The Coming*

Race. Bulwer's was no Sunday School piety. The ugly
old hag has a valid point, against Hilda, the noble
Dane.

The will theme pervades much nineteenth century
literature and philosophy. For Bulwer, the will is
especially interesting when it takes a maleficent form,
for it is precisely this energy that yields the highest
results when sublimated. The fascination with the
daemonic will is a vital thread through tales like
*Zanoni, The Haunted and the Haunters, A Strange
Story*, and *The Coming Race*.

As Bertrand Russell wrote in *The History of Western
Philosophy*, it was Schopenhauer who 'began the
emphasis on Will which is characteristic of much
nineteenth and twentieth century philosophy'.
Schopenhauer identified the will as the Kantian thing-
in-itself, so it may truly be said that for him everything
is will. Schopenhauer's influence on the art and
literature of the later nineteenth century was immense,
and so it has been suggested that perhaps Bulwer,
familiar as he was with contemporary German
literature, may have read his work. He is known to have
read Hegel, and that might be thought to show in the
dialectical nature of his historical novels.

However there is apparently no convincing evidence
that he had read Schopenhauer. Another suggested
source for the will theme is Balzac, who also wrote
mystical and occult novels. Louis Lambert,
otherworldly hero of the novel of the same name, wrote
at the age of 15 *A Treatise on the Will*, which was
discovered and destroyed by his teachers. This passage
was said to be autobiographical, a truthful account of
something that had happened to Balzac himself. In this
book Balzac preaches a strange mystical doctrine of the
omnipotence of will and thought, intended as the
crowning philosophy of the comedie humaine. Will is
so important that facts are a secondary consideration.
Doctrines of will go back far into esoteric tradition.
Balzac immersed himself in esoteric and magical
literature but then so did Bulwer himself. As he wrote

Appendix 3

to his friend Forster. "I know by experience that those wizard old books are full of holes and pitfalls. I myself once fell into one and remained there 45 days and 3 hours without food, crying for help as loud as I could, but nobody came. You may believe that or not just as you please, but its true".

Evelyn Underhill in her book on Mysticism first published in 1911, writes in a chapter on magic, which she opposes to mysticism:-

"According to its modern teachers, magic is in essence simply an extension of the theory and practice of volition beyond the usual limits . The will, says the occultist, is king, not only of the house of Life but of the universes outside the gates of sense. It is the key to man limitless, the true ring of Gyges which can control the forces of nature known and unknown."

Bulwer was such an occultist, and was said to have been the main channel by which occult ideas reached the English. Such ideas have long encountered resistance and disapproval. Underhill goes on to write of Eliphas Levi's system:-

"the doctrine of magic which has here been described shows us the Secret Wisdom at its best and sanest. But even on these levels it is dogged by the defects which so decisively separate the occultist from the mystic. The chief of these is the peculiar temper of mind, the cold intellectual arrogance, the intensely individual point of view which occult studies seem to induce by their conscious quest of exclusive power and knowledge and their implicit neglect of love."

"Magic even at its best extends rather than escapes the boundaries of the phenomenal world. It stands, where genuine, for that form of transcendentalism which does abnormal things but does not lead anywhere, and we are likely to fall victims to our kind of magic the moment that the declaration 'I want to Know' ousts the declaration 'I want to be' from the chief place in our consciousness".

This was not Bulwer's view of the matter. In a passage in *The Haunted and the Haunters*, speaking

presumably as himself, he disclaims belief in the supernatural. "Now, my theory is that the Supernatural is the Impossible, and that what is called supernatural is only a something in the laws of nature of which we have been hitherto ignorant." But as he wrote to Forster:-" I do believe in the substance of what used to be called Magic, that is I believe that there are persons of a peculiar temperament who can effect very extraordinary things not accounted for satisfactorily by any existent philosophy". The modern habit is to dismiss any talk of magic as tiresome mumbo jumbo. But even without the superstition and supernaturalism, there remains quite an interesting viewpoint.

An artist's personal beliefs may be sometimes be seen as irrelevant to his work. On the other hand he may well be the proponent of some kind of philosophy. Where an artist is inspired by a doctrine of the omnipresence and supremacy of will, it can be expected to have an effect on his attitude towards his art. A work of art can serve to express a zeitgeist, that can be its significance, and Schopenhauerian aesthetics have been employed to this end. But it can alternatively be used in an effort to create or control the zeitgeist. Such an artist is a form of shaman. Seeing himself thus, he may think of himself as purveying wisdom to his audience. Such was Bulwer , who hinted at Rosicrucian initiation.

Though he often writes about a malevolent form of will, this represents energy which may be turned to the good. Bulwer gave a far more positive valuation of the will than did Schopenhauer. In this he was in harmony with other exponents of the occult tradition. Aleister Crowley the twentieth century magus, whose word was Thelema, the Greek for will, and whose motto the Rabelaisian "Do what Thou Wilt shall be the whole of the Law", recommended two of Lytton's novels in the comprehensive reading list he provided in his *Magick in Theory and Practice*, *Zanoni* and *A Strange Story*.

For Schopenhauer, as for a Schopenhauerian like Thomas Hardy, the will itself was intrinsically evil, and

Appendix 3

the highest aim of life was ascetic renunciation. Such thoughts pervaded late romanticism, and all the art of the decadent movement, though they could easily slide over into their opposite. The most famous reversal of the negative valuation was of course the life affirmation of Nietzsche. When Nietzsche began to be discovered in England people looked for precursors in English literature, and one of those hit upon was Bulwer. One who pointed out the similarities was Alfred Orage, Nietzschean editor of the influential periodical The New Age. I quote from David Thatcher's *Nietzsche in England.*

"for Alfred Richard Orage Nietzsche was above all a mystic whose affinities with the mystical tradition were beyond all question. Nietzsche's superman, he believed, had a forebear in Mejnour, the occult superman of Bulwer-Lytton's Zanoni (!842): *'Mejnour is justifying his sacrifice of thousands of aspirants for the sake of a single success. He is inspired in this, he says, by "the hope to form a mighty and numerous race... that may proceed in their deathless destinies from stage to stage of celestial glory, and rank at last among the nearest ministrants and angels gathered round the Throne of Thrones.".. such an ideal can be paralleled perhaps in the work of a real man, singularly like Mejnour in his apparent chilly isolation, and singularly like him too in his passionate devotion to humanity - Frederic [sic] Nietzsche and the parallel is almost complete when one finds Mejnour saying of himself "my art is to make man above mankind"*

Orage was to end his career as a follower of Gurdjieff. Here is another Nietzschean thought from Zanoni:-
"*A nation that aspires to equality is unfit for freedom. Throughout all creation, from the archangel to the worm, from Olympus to the pebble from the radiant and completed planet to the nebula that hardens through ages of mist and slime into the habitable world, the first law of nature is inequality.*"
Though Bulwer's philosophy of will was not exactly Schopenhauerian, there were parallels and

connections. One of those influenced by Schopenhauer was Richard Wagner, who was also, as we know, inspired by Bulwer himself. Wagner, too, took will philosophy in the direction of magic, while following Schopenhauer closely. In his autobiography Wagner writes of enthusiastically reading Bulwer-Lytton's novels while living in Riga in the late 1830s. Apparently these were a significant influence upon him. Arguably he would try to do in his own way the same kind of thing Bulwer did in novels like Harold.

In *Harold* Bulwer is engaged in the sort of mythmaking that Wagner practised, like others after him. He exercises his own will upon the material of history. Harold himself is presented as the embodiment of nationality, of the English race.

The novel, has considerable interest, whatever its shortcomings as literature. As with all Bulwer's works it is rich in intellectual ideas. Presented as a romance, it may appear to transcend the genre. Macaulay actually described it as closer to history than romance. (This comment may say a lot about Macaulay's own attitude to his subject). Taken as history *Harold* reveals clearly the selective nature of historical interpretation. The subject matter is so vast that much has to be forgotten. But Bulwer does more than omit. He modifies his sources to give King Harold an altogether more heroic character. For the historian Sir Francis Palgrave, for example, Harold was a perjurer and sinner, virtually a usurper, in a decadent and fragmented country. Bulwer's themes of freedom, nationality and race were very powerful ones at the time. In exploring and developing them he enters a field in which epic poetry may be as effective as history proper, if not more so. *Harold* is in some respects like an epic poem. Indeed Bulwer says in the introduction that the Norman Conquest was our own Trojan War.

Writing epic to create national identity was a common enough activity at a time when some nations were in still in the process of being invented. *Harold* was published in 1848, the year of nationalist revolutions.

Appendix 3

Whatever there is to be said for enjoying a secure sense of national identity, for the magician there is something more exciting about exercising the power to invent one. His object is not to embrace a myth, but to control and direct it.

In *Harold* Bulwer discusses English ideas of freedom. He writes of Hildebrand's campaign to reform Christendom, and the papal sanctioning of the Norman invasion which made it a proto-crusade. We are told that this gave rise to a lasting sense of resentment against the papacy. Bulwer's view of history is clearly Protestant. He finds the roots of English ideas of freedom in anti-French feeling, and the constant need to resist France. He maintains that it was only the liberty among the Norman barons that permitted its eventual restoration among the English. *"Nothing is strong of earth but will"* may also be taken as an allusion to the eventual consequences of the invasion. In 1851, three years after the publication of Harold, appeared Sir Edward Creasy's *Fifteen Decisive Battles of the World*. Here is his judgment on the effects of the Battle of Hastings:-

"It may sound paradoxical, but it is in reality no exaggeration to say, with Guizot, that England owes her liberties to her having been conquered by the Normans. It is true that the Saxon institutions were the primitive cradle of English liberty, but by their own intrinsic force they could never have founded the enduring free English constitution. It was the Conquest that infused into them a new virtue; and the political liberties of England arose from the situation in which the Anglo-Saxon and the Anglo-Norman populations and laws found themselves placed relatively to each other in this island.

The state of England under her last Anglo-Saxon kings closely resembled the state of France under the last Carlovingian, and the first Capetian princes. The crown was feeble, the great nobles were strong and turbulent. And although there was more national unity in Saxon England than in France; although the English local free institutions had more reality and energy than was the case with anything analogous to them on the Continent in the eleventh century, still the probability is that the Saxon system of polity, if left to itself, would have fallen into utter confusion, out of which would have arisen first an aristocratic hierarchy like that which arose in France, next an absolute monarchy, and finally a series of anarchical revolutions, such as we now behold around, but not among us. [See Guizot, UT SUPRA.]

The latest conquerors of this island were also the bravest and the best. I do not except even the Romans. And, in spite of our sympathies with Harold and Hereward, and our abhorrence of the founder of the New Forest, and the desolator of Yorkshire, we must confess the superiority of the Normans to the Anglo-Saxons and Anglo-Danes, whom they met here in 1066, as well as to the degenerate Frank noblesse and the crushed and servile Romanesque provincials, from whom, in 912, they had wrested the district in the north of Gaul which still bears the name of Normandy.

It was not merely by extreme valour and ready subordination or military discipline, that the Normans were pre-eminent among all the conquering races of the Gothic stock, but also by their instinctive faculty of appreciating and adopting the superior civilizations which they encountered. Thus Duke Rollo and his Scandinavian warriors readily embraced the creed, the language, the laws, and the arts which France, in those troubled and evil times with which the Capetian dynasty commenced, still inherited from imperial Rome and imperial Charlemagne. They adopted the customs, the duties, the obedience that the capitularies of emperors and kings had established; but that which they brought to the application of those laws, was the spirit of life, the spirit of liberty--the habits also of military subordination, and the aptness for a state politic, which could reconcile the security of all with the

Appendix 3

independence of each. [Sismondi, Histoire des Francais, vol. iii. p. 174.] So also in all chivalric feelings, in enthusiastic religious zeal, in almost idolatrous respect to females of gentle birth, in generous fondness for the nascent poetry of the time, in a keen intellectual relish for subtle thought and disputation, in a taste for architectural magnificence, and all courtly refinement and pageantry, the Normans were the Paladins of the world. Their brilliant qualities were sullied by many darker traits of pride, of merciless cruelty, and of brutal contempt for the industry, the rights, and the feelings of all whom they considered the lower classes of mankind. Their gradual blending with the Saxons softened these harsh and evil points of their national character, and in return they fired the duller Saxon mass with a new spirit of animation and power. As Campbell boldly expressed it, "THEY HIGH-METTLED THE BLOOD OF OUR VEINS." Small had been the figure which England made in the world before the coming over of the Normans; and without them she never would have emerged from insignificance. The authority of Gibbon may be taken as decisive when he pronounces that, "Assuredly England was a gainer by the Conquest." and we may proudly adopt the comment of the Frenchman Rapin, who, writing of the battle of Hastings more than a century ago, speaks of the revolution effected by it, as "the first step by which England has arrived to that height of grandeur and glory we behold it in at present." [Rapin, Hist. England, p. 164. See also Sharon Turner, vol. iv. p. 72; and, above all, Palgrave's Normandy and England.]

This seems not far from Bulwer's own view.
As well as the theme of the conquered conquering the conquerors, the survival of Norse paganism among the Danish part of the population gave scope for something like a Gotterdamerung theme, the Twilight of the Gods, the Ragnarok, the tragic spirit from the Norse sagas. Bulwer could not resist inventing the figure of Hilda the Danish Vala, the pagan prophetess. This offers another parallel with Wagner. It dovetails nicely with another, more Christian sub-plot, the tragedy of the unconsummated love between Harold and Edith Swanneck, Hilda's ward. Bulwer purified the original legend of Harold and his mistress in an effort of conscious and deliberate mythmaking. He sanitises it and brings the lovers to a spiritual consummation in a manner that was, he claims, more appropriate to the eleventh century than it would have been to the nineteenth. Here he was wielding the blue pencil. Harold was intended as book that could safely fall into the hands of children. In this respect Bulwer was a man of his time, in full accord with the spirit of Thomas Bowdler. However there was another very different side to his character, which perhaps shows in some of the recently restored architectural features of Knebworth. We see that he was very far from a prude when we look more closely into the nature of his esoteric beliefs.
Allegedly the word vril derives from virile, the Latin for male virility. In this connection see Schopenhauer:-
World as Will and Idea §60
"The genitals are the real focus of will and are therefore the opposite pole to the brain, the representative of knowledge.... The genitals are the life-preserving principle assuring to time endless life. In this capacity they were worshipped by the Greeks as the phallus and by the Hindus as the lingam, which are therefore the symbol of the affirmation of the will".
Similar thoughts circulated among some English scholars, where they took on an unmistakably blasphemous character. There exists a letter from Bulwer to Hargrave Jennings dated 1870 acknowledging receipt of a copy of Jennings' book on the Rosicrucians. He praises it highly, telling him that *"...no better book upon such a theme has been written, or indeed could be written unless a member of the Fraternity were to break the vow which enjoins him to secrecy..."*

Appendix 3

It is most revealing that Bulwer should endorse such a work. Jennings' book on esoteric religion, art and literature, was attacked by contemporary, and some modern, critics, for what one called its "*unwholesome current*" of indecent innuendo. It gives a view of religion that is quite remote from orthodox Christianity, however attuned to certain aspects of Hinduism. Christian tradition is interpreted in a most subversive way, as full of sexual symbolism. This is taken so far as to give the cross itself an essentially phallic significance, corresponding to the lingam of the Indian Saivites. Nineteenth century English Rosicrucianism was, from a respectable point of view, quite scandalously heterodox.

Madame Blavatsky wrote a pamphlet against phallicism, which she saw as an attempt to undermine theosophy. She herself was said to owe her inspiration first to *The Last Days of Pompeii*, and later *Zanoni*. In turn she was to inspire some of the greatest modern artists. Gauguin, Mondrian, Kandinsky, Klee, Pollock, and Max Beckmann, were all at various times disciples of her theosophy.

In all this talk of will and creativity, it should not be overlooked that a book like *Harold* might perform a very different, more melancholy, function, that of consolation in defeat. The mystically inclined Emperor Napoleon III was to get to know both Bulwer and Hargrave Jennings while living in exile in England following the catastrophe of the Franco-Prussian war. He told Bulwer that he had read *Harold* on the night before surrendering his sword to William, King of Prussia, on 2nd September 1870, and that he kept it on his bedside table for several days afterwards. One year later William was to be proclaimed Kaiser of the new German Empire at Versailles.

Index

Index

Index

Index

Lightning Source UK Ltd.
Milton Keynes UK
UKHW05f1003070918
328446UK00009B/73/P